Chinua Achebe's

Things Fall Apart

Text by
Sara Talis O'Brien
(M.A., College of William and Mary; Ed.D., Rutgers University)
Associate Professor
Rivier College
Nashua, New Hampshire

Illustrations by
Karen Pica

 Research & Education Association
Dr. M. Fogiel, Director

MAXnotes® for
THINGS FALL APART

Printed in the United States of America

Library of Congress Catalog Card Number 98-66037

International Standard Book Number 0-87891-233-9

MAXnotes® is a registered trademark of
Research & Education Association, Piscataway, New Jersey 08854

What **MAXnotes**® *Will Do for You*

This book is intended to help you absorb the essential contents and features of Achebe's *Things Fall Apart* and to help you gain a thorough understanding of the work. The book has been designed to do this more quickly and effectively than any other study guide.

For best results, this **MAXnotes** book should be used as a companion to the actual work, not instead of it. The interaction between the two will greatly benefit you.

To help you in your studies, this book presents the most up-to-date interpretations of every section of the actual work, followed by questions and fully explained answers that will enable you to analyze the material critically. The questions also will help you to test your understanding of the work and will prepare you for discussions and exams.

Meaningful illustrations are included to further enhance your understanding and enjoyment of the literary work. The illustrations are designed to place you into the mood and spirit of the work's settings.

The **MAXnotes** also include summaries, character lists, explanations of plot, and section-by-section analyses. A biography of the author and discussion of the work's historical context will help you put this literary piece into the proper perspective of what is taking place.

The use of this study guide will save you the hours of preparation time that would ordinarily be required to arrive at a complete grasp of this work of literature. You will be well-prepared for classroom discussions, homework, and exams. The guidelines that are included for writing papers and reports on various topics will prepare you for any added work which may be assigned.

The **MAXnotes** will take your grades "to the max."

Dr. Max Fogiel
Program Director

Contents

> **Each chapter includes List of Characters, Summary,
> Analysis, Study Questions and Answers, and
> Suggested Essay Topics.**

MAXnotes® are simply the best – but don't just take our word for it...

"... I have told every bookstore in the area to carry your MAXnotes. They are the only notes I recommend to my students. There is no comparison between MAXnotes and all other notes ..."
  – High School Teacher & Reading Specialist, Arlington High School, Arlington, MA

"... I discovered the MAXnotes when a friend loaned me her copy of the MAXnotes for Romeo and Juliet. The book really helped me understand the story. Please send me a list of stores in my area that carry the MAXnotes. I would like to use more of them ..."
  – Student, San Marino, CA

"... The two MAXnotes titles that I have used have been very, very useful in helping me understand the subject matter reviewed. Thank you for creating the MAXnotes series ..."
  – Student, Morrisville, PA

AFRICA

This map divides Africa into North, East, West, Central, and Southern regions.

Map by Daniel Marino

NIGERIA

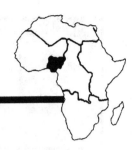

Kano

Komadugu Gana River

Maiduguri

Mubi

Kainji Lake

Abuja

Niger River

Benue River

Ibada Ife

Lagos

Benin City

Enug

Onitsha Aba

Port Harcour

0 150 kilometers

0 miles

Chinua Achebe writes about the Igbo people of Nigeria. Igbo is one of over 250
languages spoken in modern Nigeria.

Map by Daniel Marino

A Glance at Some of the Characters

Okonkwo

Ikemefuna

Ojiugo

Chielo

Uchendu

Mr. Brown

Egwugwu

Ekwefi

Introduction

The Life and Work of Chinua Achebe

Chinua Achebe is one of Africa's most influential writers. *Things Fall Apart*, Achebe's first novel, was published in 1958, just before Nigeria gained independence. The title of the novel echoes W. B. Yeats's poem "The Second Coming," which describes history as a succession of gyres, or spirals. Achebe applies the image to Africa as the nineteenth century traditional world of the Igbo people gives way to the colonial forces of the twentieth century.

Things Fall Apart is based upon Achebe's life experience. Born in 1930, Chinua Achebe spent his early childhood in Ogidi, Nigeria, a large village near the famous marketplace of Onitsha. Achebe was a child of both the traditional Igbo world and the colonial Christian world, because his father, Isaiah Achebe, worked as a catechist for the Church Missionary Society. Although Achebe spoke Igbo at home, he studied English in school. At the age of 14, he advanced to the prestigious Government College in Umuahia.

In 1948, Achebe was awarded a scholarship to study medicine at the University College in Ibadan. However, he soon refocused his program on literature, religion, and history. Achebe was repelled by the fundamental racism of colonial classics such as Joseph Conrad's *Heart of Darkness* and Joyce Cary's *Mister Johnson*. These novels depicted a savage Africa that was humanized only through European colonialism. In reaction, Achebe expanded his own understanding of the Igbo world with a study of oral accounts and written colonial records; he also published his first essays, editorials, and short stories as the student editor of the *University Herald*.

After graduation, Achebe taught for a brief period. In 1954, he took a position with the Nigerian Broadcasting Corporation, and from 1961–1966, he served as the director of external broadcasting. As Nigeria moved toward independence, Achebe's radio programs helped shape a national identity. During this time, Achebe also wrote his first four novels and became the founding editor of Heinemann Publisher's "African Writers Series." *Things Fall Apart* was followed by *No Longer at Ease* (1960), *Arrow of God* (1964), and *A Man of the People* (1966).

In 1967, Achebe supported Biafra's secession from Nigeria and left broadcasting to pursue research at the University of Nigeria. His reflections about the civil war were published as *Beware Soul Brother and Other Poems* (1971) and *Girls at War and Other Stories* (1972). His essays were published as *Morning Yet on Creation Day* (1975); *The Trouble with Nigeria* (1983); and *Hopes and Impediments: Selected Essays, 1965–87* (1988). His essays have had a great influence on contemporary thought about Africa and African literature. For example, "The Novelist as Teacher" explains the role of the writer in Africa, and "The African Writer and the English Language" explains Achebe's use of language. These essays are among his most often quoted essays, and they are included in *Morning Yet on Creation Day*. Achebe also coedited *Don't Let Him Die: An Anthology of Memorial Poems for Christopher Okigbo* (1978), and founded *Okike: An African Journal of New Writing*.

Achebe has also written several children's books, including *Chike and the River* (1966), *The Drum* (1977), and *The Flute* (1977). He has also edited *African Short Stories* (1982) and *The Heinemann Book of Contemporary African Stories* (1992). Finally, Achebe published his fifth novel, *Anthills of the Savannah*, in 1987.

In addition to his research and writing, over the past 20 years Chinua Achebe has worked as a professor of literature, the director of African Studies, and a pro-vice-chancellor at the University of Nigeria. He has also served as a distinguished visiting professor of literature at the University of Massachusetts, the University of Connecticut, City College of New York, and Bard College. Achebe has lectured extensively throughout Africa and the United States, and he has received numerous awards, including the Nigerian

National Merit Award. Chinua Achebe has influenced many African writers through his writing and his work as the chairperson of the Society of Nigerian Authors.

Historical Background

A distinctive culture known as Igbo (or Ibo) evolved in West Africa about 5,000 years ago. In the traditional worldview, the Creator God Chukwu was a remote masculine force who taught the people to survive through the cultivation of yams. The yam stood as an indicator of wealth and a type of currency. The masculine Chukwu was balanced by the Earth goddess Ani, or Mother Nature. The feminine Ani was closer to humankind than Chukwu, for she functioned as the goddess of fertility and the judge of morality.

These great masculine and feminine creative forces were augmented by localized deities, spirits, and oracles that were institutionalized by various Igbo communities. Each oracle spoke through a priest or priestess and served as a medium through which the divine was understood. The Igbo further personified the power of God in the concept of the *chi*. The *chi* was the personalized god-force or invisible power of fate that guided each individual through life. It was the finely tuned *chi* that simultaneously controlled a person's fortunes yet allowed the individual freedom to work creatively toward success or failure.

Political organizations and beliefs differed among the various groups of Igbo people. Historically, many Igbo villages were representative democracies bound to a group of villages by the decisions of a general assembly. The local life of each village was shaped by age-grade associations, title-making societies, work associations, religious fraternities, and secret societies. Men and women attempted to achieve prestige and status by accumulating wealth, which was used to purchase titles. Title-holding leaders influenced the village assembly, came to decisions through consensus, made new laws, and administered justice.

Early on, the Igbo people developed relationships with European traders and missionaries. In 1472, the Portuguese arrived in Igboland in an attempt to discover a sea route to India; in 1508, the Portuguese transported the first West African slaves to the West Indies. The slave trade flourished for three centuries; however, the Igbo also traded copper rods, iron bars, and cowrie shells with the Portuguese and the Dutch over the next two centuries. The slave trade was abolished in 1807, and the Igbo began to trade palm oil with the British. The Anglican Church Missionary Society established a mission in Onitsha in 1857; later the Roman Catholic Holy Ghost Fathers and Society of African Missions set up stations east and west of the Niger River.

Friendly relations with Britain crumbled after 1875. Although Igboland had functioned as a British trade colony for decades, it was not formally declared a British Protectorate until 1900. In order to "pacify" Eastern Nigeria, the British destroyed much of Igboland and launched extensive military expeditions in 1914. Despite resistance, by 1928 Igbo men were forced to pay taxes, and British colonialism took hold.

During the colonial era, British officials sought to govern hundreds of decentralized Igbo villages clustered in various political constructs through a system of indirect rule. Igbo institutions were replaced with a native court system that was administered by appointed warrant chiefs, district officers, court clerks, and messengers who held no traditional status in the village. The Igbo resisted the corruption of the native court system, the destruction of indigenous political life, and increased taxation. The resistance culminated in the Women's War of 1929–1930. Women throughout Nigeria demanded social reforms, respect for Igbo customs, and women's rights. In the final analysis, their action forced the British to restructure Eastern Nigeria to comply more closely with traditional village organization.

In 1952, a regional government was set up which paved the way for independence. After decades of resistance, Nigeria finally gained independence from Britain in 1960. However, the new nation contained many ethnic groups, including the Hausa and the Yoruba people. The eastern region of Nigeria was inhabited by the Igbo. This area, which was later known as Biafra, unsuccessfully sought independence from Nigeria during the devastating civil war of 1966–1969.

Things Fall Apart depicts the tensions within traditional Igbo society at the end of the nineteenth century and the cataclysmic changes introduced by colonialism and Christianity in the twentieth century. Chinua Achebe writes in English; however, in order to recreate the cultural milieu of the Igbo people, he "Africanizes" the language of the novel. Specific Igbo words and complicated names are used freely. Profound philosophical concepts such as *chi* and *ogbanje* are explained in the text or glossary and are fundamental to the story. The use of idioms and proverbs also clarifies the conflict, expresses different points of view, and instructs the characters as well as the reader. *Things Fall Apart* has been translated into 30 languages and has sold 8 million copies. The novel is internationally acclaimed, has become a classic of African literature, and has served as a seminal text for postcolonial literature around the world.

Master List of Major Characters

Okonkwo—*the protagonist; a strong, proud, hardworking Igbo*

Obierika—*Okonkwo's confidant; he refuses to participate in killing Ikemefuna*

Ikemefuna—*a boy taken from Mbaino as a compensation for murder*

Ani—*the Earth goddess who calls for Ikemefuna's death*

Unoka—*Okonkwo's father; he loves to play the flute and appears to be lazy*

Nwoye—*Okonkwo's eldest son; he takes the Christian name Isaac*

Ekwefi—*Okonkwo's second wife; mother of Ezinma*

Ezinma—*Ekwefi's only daughter*

Agbala—*Oracle of the Hills and Caves*

Chielo—*Agbala's priestess; she is a widow with two children*

Nwoye's mother—*Okonkwo's first wife; she is very strong*

Ojiugo—*Okonkwo's youngest wife, who is beaten during the Week of Peace*

Uchendu—*Okonkwo's uncle; his mother's brother and the elder in Mbanta*

Ezeudu (Ogbuefi Ezeudu)—*an elder and a friend of Okonkwo*

Nwakibie—*an important man in Umuofia; he helps Okonkwo begin his farm*

Ndulue—*a respected elder who dies shortly before his beloved wife Ozoemena*

Ozoemena—*Ndulue's wife; she dies shortly after her husband*

Mr. Brown—*a European missionary based in Umuofia*

Mr. Kiaga—*an Igbo missionary in charge of the congregation in Mbanta*

Mr. Smith—*a zealous, rigid missionary who takes over for Mr. Brown*

District Commissioner—*the British official in charge of Igboland*

Enoch—*a zealous Christian*

Okoli—*a convert to Christianity who kills the sacred python and dies*

Chukwu—*the supreme Creator God of the Igbo traditional religion*

Minor Characters

Akueke—*Obierika's daughter; her marriage is negotiated*

Amalinze—*called the Cat; a great wrestler who is thrown by Okonkwo*

Anene—*Ekwefi's first husband*

Chika—*Agbala's priestess during Unoka's time*

Ezeani—*the priest of the Earth goddess*

Ezeugo—*a powerful orator*

Maduka—*Obierika's son; a great wrestler*

Obiageli—*Nwoye's sister*

Ogbuefi Udo—*his wife is murdered by the people of Mbaino*

Okagbue—*the medicine man who destroys Ezinma's* iyi-uwa

Okeke—*the interpreter for Mr. Smith*

Okoye—*a neighbor who unsuccessfully tries to collect a debt from Unoka*

Osugo—*a man without titles*

Glossary

Note: The "o" in Igbo words is pronounced "aw" as in "awesome."

agadi-nwayi—*an old woman*

agbala—*a woman, the term is an insult to a man because it implies weakness*

Amadioha—*the god of thunder and lightning*

bride-price—*a dowry paid by the groom's parents to the bride's parents*

chi—*the god-force within each person; an individual's character, destiny, or fate*

cowries—*shells used as money*

diala—*a freeborn individual*

efulefu—*a worthless man*

egwugwu—*leaders dressed as masked spirits representing the ancestors*

ekwe—*a wooden drum*

eneke-nti-oba—*a bird*

eze-agadi-nwayi—*an old woman's teeth*

foo foo—*a pounded yam dish*

harmattan—*a dry wind from the north*

iba—*a fever*

Iguedo—*Okonkwo's village*

ikenga—*a wooden carving containing a man's personal spirit*

ilo—*the village playground or common where meetings are held*

inyanga—*showing off; bragging*

isa-ifi—a ceremony determining a woman's faithfulness to her fiancé after a long separation

iyi-uwa—a sacred stone that links the ogbanje *child with the spirit world*

jigida—a string of waist beads

kite—a bird that arrives during the dry season

kola nuts—nuts offered to guests as a symbol of hospitality

kotma—a court man or court messenger

kwenu—a greeting

ndichie—the elders who meet in a judicial council

nna ayi—our father

nno—welcome

nso-ani—a taboo or religious offense

nza—a small bird

obi—the living quarters of the head of a family

obodo dike—the land of the brave

ochu—murder or manslaughter

ogbanje—a child who dies and returns to his/her mother's womb to be reborn

ogene—a gong

osu—a person dedicated to a god; a slave and an outcast

otu omu—a women's council that controls the marketplace by imposing fines on anyone who disturbs the peace

Oye—one of the four market days

ozo—one of the titles a man could achieve

palm wine—a fermented beverage made from palm tree sap

tufia—a curse

udu—a type of drum

umuada—a gathering of daughters in a family

umunna—*the extended family*

Umuofia—*Okonkwo's clan, consisting of nine villages*

uri—*part of a betrothal ceremony where the bride-price is paid*

Summary of the Novel

Things Fall Apart is a story told by a skillful storyteller. The novel attempts to recreate the social, cultural, and religious fabric of traditional Igbo life between 1850 and the early 1900s. However, the novel cannot be interpreted as an accurate social and political history of the Igbo people, because it is a work of fiction. Nevertheless, the novel depicts conflicts and tensions within Igbo society as well as changes introduced by colonial rule and Christianity. The novel is structured in three parts. Part One depicts life in pre-colonial Igboland. Part Two relates the arrival of the Europeans and the introduction of Christianity, and Part Three recounts the beginning of systematic colonial control in eastern Nigeria. Okonkwo, the protagonist, is a talented but inflexible Igbo who struggles to achieve success in the traditional world.

The setting of Part One is Umuofia, a union of nine villages. Okonkwo is introduced as a great wrestler, a renowned warrior, and a hardworking member of the community. He has amassed two barns filled with yams, three wives, many children, and two titles. His goal is to move through the traditional Igbo title-taking system by balancing personal achievement and community service. However, although Okonkwo feels he *is* destined for greatness, his *chi*, or the god-force within him, *does not seem destined for greatness*.

Okonkwo seeks to overpower his mediocre *chi* by working hard. He is profoundly afraid of failure. As a result, he is unable to balance the feminine energy of love with the masculine energy of material success. Okonkwo often suppresses his feminine side as he pursues his goals and angers the Earth goddess Ani. His rage, inflexibility, and fear of appearing weak like his lazy father, the musician Unoka, consistently overshadow his respect for his community.

When a daughter of Umuofia is killed by the neighboring village of Mbaino, a young boy named Ikemefuna is given to Umuofia

in order to avoid war. Okonkwo adopts the boy and seems to ad-
mire him, for Ikemefuna is both a talented musician and a great
hunter. He is also a brother and role model for Okonkwo's eldest
son Nwoye, who appears to be lazy. Ikemefuna lives with Okonkwo
for three years until the Oracle of the Hills and Caves demands
his life. Ogbuefi Ezeudu, the oldest man in the village, advises
Okonkwo not to take part in the ritual killing of the boy. Although
Okonkwo loves Ikemefuna, he does not want to appear weak. He
joins the ceremony and kills Ikemefuna. Okonkwo's action ulti-
mately shatters his relationship with his sensitive son, Nwoye.

   Okonkwo is both affectionate and violent with his family. He
loves his daughter Ezinma, who is an *ogbanje*, or a changeling child
who seems to die continually only to return to her mother's womb
to be reborn and die again. In an attempt to break the power of the
ogbanje, Okonkwo follows his wife Ekwefi, the priestess Chielo, and
his daughter Ezinma on a journey to the oracle Agbala. Okonkwo
also assists a medicine man locate and destroy his daughter's
iyi-uwa, or the sacred stone that links the child with the spirit world.
However, Okonkwo also has a dark and dangerous side, for he controls his family through anger. In bouts of rage, he beats his youngest wife, Ojiugo, for neglecting to cook dinner and braiding her hair
instead during the Week of Peace. He also takes a shot at Ekwefi
with a rusty gun during the Yam Festival.

   Okonkwo's immoral actions affect the community. During the
funeral rite for the elder Ezeudu, Okonkwo's gun accidentally ex-
plodes, killing Ezeudu's son. Okonkwo's crimes enrage the Earth
Goddess Ani, for he has consciously and unconsciously chosen
death by beating his wife, killing Ikemefuna, and now, killing
Ezeudu's son. His irrational actions are destroying the moral fabric of traditional life. Therefore, Ani banishes Okonkwo to Mbanta,
his mother's village, for seven years.

   Part Two of the novel takes place while Okonkwo is in exile in
Mbanta. Okonkwo flees to his mother's village and takes refuge with
the feminine principal represented by the Earth goddess. He is
given time to learn the supremacy of a mother's nurturing love.
However, Okonkwo's goals never change. He works hard to amass
wealth through the production of yams, and he dreams of returning to Umuofia to become a judicial leader in the clan. While

Okonkwo single-mindedly labors in Mbanta, the Europeans arrive in Igboland. His friend Obierika visits him twice with news of the political and social upheaval. Abame, one of the villages in the union of Umuofia, is razed by the British. Christianity, a new religion, is attracting the marginal members of the Igbo community. The disenfranchised among the Igbo include the anguished mothers of twins who are forced to discard their children in the Evil Forest, the *osu*, who are despised descendants of religious slave cults, and unsuccessful men who do not earn titles or achieve status in the traditional world. The new Christian converts include Okonkwo's son, Nwoye.

In Part Three, Okonkwo returns from exile in Mbanta to a tense and radically changed Umuofia. At this point, a colonial government is taking root, the palm-oil trade is transforming the economy, and Christianity is dividing the Igbo people. Tensions escalate at the annual worship of the Earth goddess when the zealous Christian convert Enoch unmasks an *egwugwu*, a masquerader representing an ancestral spirit. His apostasy kills the spirit, unmasks the traditional religion, and throws Umuofia into confusion. Other *egwugwu*, who are actually Igbo men masked as ancestors, are enraged and retaliate. They raze Enoch's compound to the ground and burn the new Christian church. Okonkwo and other village leaders are subsequently jailed and whipped by order of the District Commissioner. After paying a fine, the humiliated Igbo are released from prison.

The traditional Igbo gather to mourn the abominations suffered by the ancient gods, the ancestors, and the entire Igbo community. They decry the new religion, which has pitted Igbo against Igbo. When colonial officials arrive to disperse the crowd, Okonkwo blocks them. He draws his machete and decapitates the court messenger. Okonkwo marshals no support; however, for the divided Igbo community fails to rise in defense of traditional life. Okonkwo has no recourse. He retreats and hangs himself from a tree.

Okonkwo fails to achieve immortality according to Igbo tradition. Only strangers may touch him now, for he has committed suicide, the ultimate offense against the Earth goddess. Okonkwo does not even merit a simple burial among his own people. In the final denouement, a perplexed District Commissioner orders members of the Igbo community to appear in court with Okonkwo's corpse. The commissioner decides to allot the tragedy of Okonkwo a paragraph in his anthropological study of the Igbo, which he has cruelly entitled "The Pacification of the Primitive Tribes of the Lower Niger." (p. 148)

Although the novel represents Igboland in the 1890s, it is crucial for the reader to remember that Achebe wrote *Things Fall Apart* in 1958, at the dawn of Nigerian independence. Achebe writes from a realistic third person point of view and questions assumptions about civilization, culture, and literature. Proverbs, folk tales, myths, and portraits of rituals and festivals support the basic plot line and paint a picture of Igbo life. In *Morning Yet on Creation Day*, Achebe explains his desire to show that precolonial Africa was "not one long nightmare of savagery." (p. 45) Overall, Achebe succeeds in presenting Igbo society as an organic whole and providing a window into the heart of Africa.

Estimated Reading Time

Things Fall Apart is approximately 150 pages long. Reading time depends upon your reading level. You will read faster as you become familiar with Chinua Achebe's style. Thirty to thirty-five pages may be covered in an hour's sitting. The book may be completed in approximately seven to eight hours.

SECTION TWO

Part One

Chapter One

New Characters:

Okonkwo: *famous in the nine villages of Umuofia for his personal achievements*

Amalinze: *the Cat; the greatest wrestler in Umuofia*

Unoka: *Okonkwo's father; he is a lazy debtor*

Okoye: *Unoka's neighbor who attempts to collect a debt*

Ikemefuna: *a young boy who is given to Umuofia by a rival village*

Summary

Okonkwo is a man of great personal achievements. After he threw the great wrestler Amalinze the Cat, at the age of 18, his fame spread. He is a wealthy farmer with three wives, many children, two barns full of yams, and two titles. He has also proven his prowess in two intertribal wars. Because he is so well respected, Okonkwo is chosen to adopt the ill-fated lad Ikemefuna, who is given to the community of Umuofia by the village of Mbaino in order to avoid war and bloodshed.

Unoka, Okonkwo's father, loves to drink palm wine and play the flute. He is poor, and his wife and children barely have food to eat. Unoka never repays his loans, and the people laugh at him.

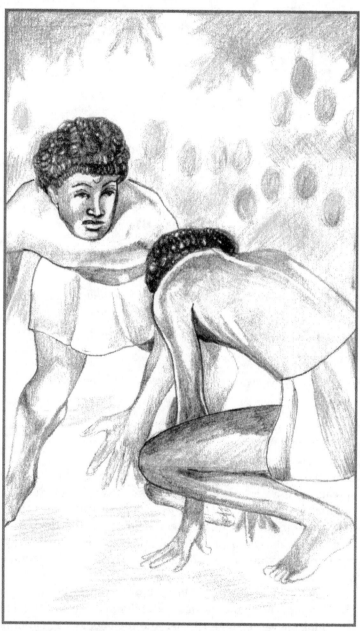

As a young man, Okonkwo throws the great wrestler Amalinze the Cat, and his fame spreads throughout the nine villages of Umuofia.

When Unoka dies, he holds no title, and he is heavily in debt. Okonkwo is ashamed of him.

Unoka welcomes his neighbor Okoye by breaking open the kola nut, which is a symbol of hospitality. The men talk about the rains, the upcoming feasts, and the impending wars. Okoye reminds Unoka that he will soon take the Idemili title, which is the third highest title in the land. This is an expensive ceremony. Okoye speaks indirectly through proverbs and then finally asks Unoka to return the 200 cowries he borrowed more than two years ago. Unoka bursts out laughing and tells Okoye that the walls of his house are covered with strokes marking debts of 100 cowries he owes to various people in the community. Unoka tells Okoye that he will pay him someday but that he will pay his big debts first.

Analysis

Okonkwo is famous because of his "solid personal achievements." (p. 3) This statement is central to understanding the protagonist. Okonkwo believes he is clearly cut out for great things, for "As the elders said, if a child washed his hands, he could eat with kings." (p. 6) Okonkwo strives to succeed in the traditional Igbo world, and he stands in stark contrast to Unoka, his poor, lazy father. Okonkwo is afraid of failing and appearing weak like his father. He disdains feminine activities such as playing the flute, and he gravitates to the masculine energy in Igbo society by amassing material wealth in yams.

Both Okonkwo and Unoka stand in contrast to Okoye. Okoye is also a musician who plays an instrument called the *ogene*, or a gong. However, Okoye is not a failure like Unoka. He owns a large barn full of yams; he has three wives; and he is preparing to take the expensive Idemili title. This title will allow him to participate more fully in political matters of the community. Throughout the novel, Okonkwo attempts to succeed; however, unlike Okoye, he never achieves the balance between the feminine and masculine energies.

The first chapter involves the reader in Achebe's "Africanized" English. Musical instruments such as the *ekwe*, *udu*, and the *ogene* are introduced. The reader can decipher the meaning of the Igbo words by using context clues. Other Igbo words such as *egwugwu* represent concepts that the Western reader cannot understand through the context alone. The Igbo terms and concepts are defined in the novel's glossary. The reader is also introduced to several proverbs, for "Among the Igbo the art of conversation is regarded very highly, and proverbs are the palm-oil with which words are eaten." (p. 5) A careful reading of the Igbo words and concepts as well as the many Igbo proverbs sprinkled throughout the text provide an in-depth understanding of the novel.

Finally, the Igbo culture and the main character are introduced in contrast to Unoka, who chooses to be an individual or an *agbala* by following feminine energy. The litany of Okonkwo's achievements sets up the opposition between father and son and introduces a narrative and a culture defined by duality.

Study Questions

1. Why is Okonkwo's defeat of Amalinze the Cat such a great achievement?

2. Describe Okonkwo.

3. What does Unoka do with his money?

4. What is the harmattan?

5. Why does Unoka sing to the kites?

6. Why does Unoka enjoy playing music for the *egwugwu*, or the masqueraders who impersonate the ancestral spirits of the village?

7. What is the meaning of the proverb "He who brings kola brings life"? (p. 5)

8. Why is Okonkwo ashamed of his father, Unoka?

9. Compare Okonkwo with his father.

10. Why is Ikemefuna offered to the village of Umuofia?

Answers

1. The Cat, the greatest wrestler in the region, was unbeaten for seven years.

2. Okonkwo is huge with bushy eyebrows and a wide nose. He breathes heavily and seems to walk on springs as if he is about to pounce on someone. He has no patience with unsuccessful men like his father.

3. Unoka buys gourds of palm wine and drinks with his neighbors.

4. The harmattan is a dry wind that blows across West Africa from the north.

5. Unoka loves to sing a welcome to the birds, or kites, who return to the village from their long journey south.

6. Unoka enjoys eating and drinking at the feasts.

7. The kola nut is a symbol of hospitality and friendship.

8. Okonkwo's father has no titles; he is heavily in debt when he dies.

9. Okonkwo washes his hands of his father's failures and becomes a leader in the community.

10. Ikemefuna is offered to Umuofia by the neighboring village of Mbaino as a compensation in order to avoid war.

Suggested Essay Topics

1. Compare and contrast Okonkwo with his father, Unoka. Give special attention to the reasons why Okonkwo disdains his father and strives to succeed.

2. Discuss the significance of the three proverbs introduced in Chapter One. Thoroughly explain each proverb and define its meaning in the context of the chapter. What is Chinua Achebe's overall purpose in using Igbo proverbs in the novel?

Chapter Two

New Characters:

Ogbuefi Ezeugo: *a powerful orator who accuses Mbaino of murder*

Ogbuefi Udo: *a man of Umuofia; his wife is murdered by the people of Mbaino*

Nwoye: *Okonkwo's 12-year-old son, who appears to be lazy*

Summary

The *ogene*, a kind of gong, pierces the night in Umuofia. Umuofia is a community of nine Igbo villages related to one another in political matters. Every man is called to meet at the marketplace where Ogbuefi Ezeugo, a powerful orator, shouts the greeting "*Umuofia kwenu*," and 10,000 men respond "*Yaa*." In anger he explains that the wife of Ogbuefi Udo has been murdered in Mbaino, a rival village. An ultimatum is given to the people of Mbaino. They may choose war, or offer a young man and a young virgin to Umuofia as compensation for the murdered woman.

Umuofia is feared by its neighbors, and Okonkwo is sent to Mbaino as an emissary of war. He returns with a young girl and a 15-year-old boy named Ikemefuna. The elders, or the *ndichie*, decide the girl should replace Ogbuefi Udo's murdered wife. Ikemefuna, however, belongs to the clan. Because Okonkwo is a prosperous village leader, he is asked to look after Ikemefuna. The boy is terrified as he is handed over to Okonkwo's senior wife.

Okonkwo works on his farm from morning until night, and he rarely feels fatigued. He rules his household with a heavy hand. However, Okonkwo's three wives and eight children are not as strong, and they suffer. Okonkwo constantly nags and beats Nwoye, his 12-year-old son, because he appears to be lazy. Therefore, Nwoye is developing into a sad-faced youth.

Analysis

Okonkwo is depicted as a prosperous and warlike man. Okonkwo's homestead, or compound, illustrates his prosperity. His own living area is called an *obi*, and his three wives have separate

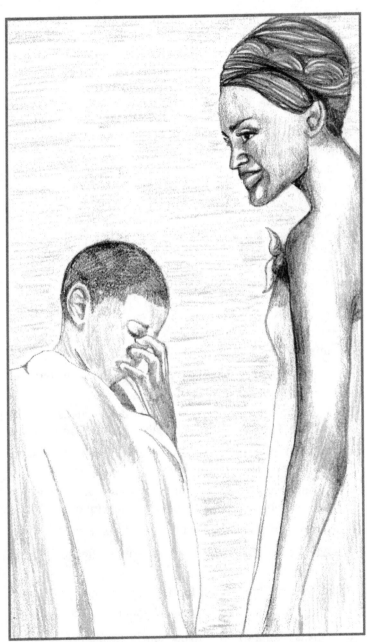

The hostage Ikemefuna is handed over to Okonkwo's senior wife.

houses behind the *obi*. The compound includes a barn with large stocks of yams, or sweet potatoes. There is also a shrine where Okonkwo keeps the symbols of his personal god and ancestral spirits. He has captured numerous human heads throughout the wars of Umuofia. Okonkwo displays his warlike nature on important occasions like funerals by drinking his palm wine from the first human head he captured in battle. Okonkwo also plays an active role in village politics. He serves as the emissary to Mbaino because he is so well respected.

Although Okonkwo appears to rule his family with an iron fist, his life is controlled by a deep-seated fear of failure; fear is also his motivation for working so hard. Okonkwo is afraid he will resemble his father, who did not earn any titles and died a miserable debtor. Okonkwo is also fearful that his eldest son, Nwoye, will be lazy like his grandfather, Unoka. Therefore, the character of Okonkwo is developed not only in contrast with Unoka, his father, but also in contrast with Nwoye, his son.

Study Questions

1. How does Okonkwo display his fierce and warlike nature at important occasions in the village?

2. Give examples illustrating the Igbo people's vague terror of darkness.

3. Why would the people of Umuofia be beaten in the war with Mbaino if they disobeyed the Oracles of the Hills and Caves?

4. Why is Ikemefuna selected by the people of Mbaino to serve as the peace sacrifice for Umuofia?

5. Okonkwo is very strong and rarely feels tired. How would you describe Okonkwo's three wives and children?

6. Why is Nwoye developing into a sad-faced youth?

7. Which one of Okonkwo's wives is the most afraid of him and why?

8. Why does Okonkwo rule his household with a heavy hand?

9. How is Unoka regarded by many members of the village?

10. Why is Okonkwo asked to become Ikemefuna's guardian?

Answers

1. Okonkwo displays his warlike nature on occasions such as funerals by drinking his palm wine from the first human head he captured in battle.

2. The Igbo people do not play in the open fields on dark and silent nights.

3. The people of Umuofia would be beaten in the war with Mbaino if they disobeyed the Oracles of the Hills and Caves because their gods would not allow them to fight a war of blame.

4. The people of Mbaino select Ikemefuna as the peace sacrifice because his father participated in murdering the woman from Umuofia in the marketplace.

5. Okonkwo's wives and children are not as strong as Okonkwo.

6. Nwoye is developing into a sad-faced youth because he is constantly nagged and beaten by his father, Okonkwo.

7. The third wife is the most afraid of Okonkwo because she is the youngest.

8. Okonkwo rules his household with a heavy hand because he wants his family to work hard and prosper. He is also afraid of appearing weak like his father.

9. The villagers think Unoka is like a weak woman because he did not earn any titles.

10. Okonkwo is asked to become Ikemefuna's guardian because he is a prosperous village leader.

Suggested Essay Topics

1. In what ways is Okonkwo a respected leader in the village? Give three examples to support your points.

2. Describe the homestead of Okonkwo, his three wives, and eight children. What does the homestead reveal about Igbo culture? Discuss three points and provide examples to support your ideas.

Chapter Three

New Characters:

Agbala: *Oracle of the Hills and Caves; a kind of god*

Chika: *the priestess to Agbala in Unoka's time*

Ani: *the Earth goddess; the owner of the land*

Ifejioku: *the god of yams*

Nwakibie: *a successful man who has taken all the titles except one in the clan*

Anasi: *one of Nwakibie's wives*

Ogbuefi Idigo: *a villager at Nwakibie's homestead*

Obiako: *a palm-wine tapper who suddenly gives up his work*

Akukalia: *a villager at Nwakibie's homestead*

Igwelo: *Nwakibie's elder son*

Summary

People like Unoka consult Agbala, the Oracle of the Hills and Caves, during times of misfortune. Chika, Agbala's priestess, tells Unoka his harvest depends upon hard work. Unoka sows yams on exhausted farms, and he does not work like a man. Unoka has a weak *chi*, or personal god. He is ill-fated, and evil fortune follows him. Therefore, Okonkwo does not inherit a barn, a title, or a young wife from his father.

Okonkwo works for Nwakibie, a highly successful man with nine wives and 30 children, who has taken all the titles in the clan except one. Okonkwo meets with Igbo men named Idigo, Akukalia, and Igwelo at Nwakibie's *obi*. They drink from a pot of palm wine and discuss village affairs. The men speak in riddles and proverbs rich in meaning. Finally, Okonkwo explains he has cleared a farm, but he has no yams to plant. He says he is not afraid of hard work. Nwakibie has refused similar requests because young farmers often neglect the yam saplings. He says, "Eneke the bird says that since men have learnt to shoot without missing, he has learnt to fly without perching." (p. 16) Like Eneke the bird, Nwakibie has learned from experience. However, Nwakibie is impressed with Okonkwo and gives him 800 yams. Okonkwo receives an additional 400 yams from one of his father's friends in Isiuzo.

That year Okonkwo sows the 400 yam seeds he has saved from his previous harvest. However, a severe drought burns the yams. When the rains return, Okonkwo plants the rest of his seed-yams. After the drought, rain pounds the earth. The harvest is like a sad funeral, and farmers weep as they dig up the rotting yams. One man hangs himself from a tree in desperation. Okonkwo remembers that tragic year the rest of his life. Unoka tells him that a proud heart can survive a general failure. As Unoka grows old and sick, his love of talk increases. It tries Okonkwo's patience.

Analysis

The religious concepts of the Oracle and the *chi* are introduced in this chapter. The Oracle straddles the religious and mundane worlds of the Igbo people and functions as a center of divination. The Oracle explains events and offers advice. Unoka is an example of an individual who consults an oracle. The *chi* is the personal god-force, the fate, or the destiny of an individual. A person's fortunes in life are more or less controlled by the *chi*. An individual's *chi* may be malicious or benevolent. A person with a good *chi* is successful. A person with a bad *chi* will achieve success only by working very hard. Unoka is a failure according to Igbo norms. He has a weak *chi*, or poor character. By using the term *chi* throughout the novel, Achebe retains the unique Igbo sense of this religious concept.

The yam is also introduced as the king of crops—a man's crop. It stands as an indication of wealth and a type of currency in Igbo society. The masculine yam is contrasted with the women's crops, which include cocoyams, beans, and cassava. Nwakibie, a prosperous Igbo farmer with a huge store of yams, is held up as an ideal Igbo. He has acquired much wealth and many titles. Men like Nwakibie play an important role in the community by helping younger men start farms through sharecropping. Okonkwo strives to become like Nwakibie, but due to the drought, his harvest is a failure. He survives the difficult year only because of his iron, inflexible will. Unoka's reminder that individual failure is more

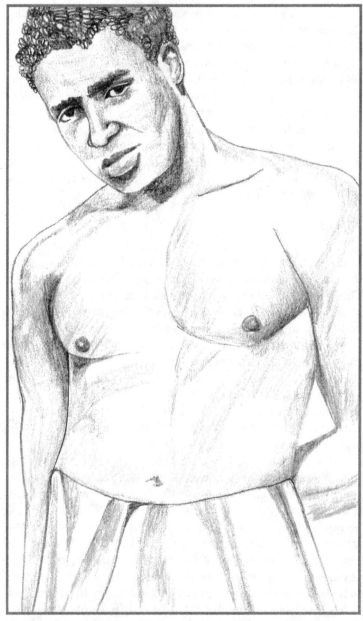

The powerful Okonkwo has no patience with unsuccessful men like his father.

bitter than the general failure of the community may serve as a curse on Okonkwo.

Study Questions

1. Why is Unoka, who dies of swelling in the stomach, abandoned and left to die in the Evil Forest?

2. Why is Nwakibie considered a successful man in Igbo society?

3. Nwakibie says, "You will have what is good for you and I will have what is good for me. Let the kite perch and let the eagle perch too. If one says no to the other, let his wing break." (p. 14) What is the meaning of Nwakibie's words?

4. What is the meaning of the proverb "A toad does not run in the daytime for nothing"? (p. 15)

5. Why does Okonkwo laugh uneasily at the story of Obiako and the oracle?

6. What is the meaning of the proverb "The lizard that jumped from the high iroko tree to the ground said he would praise himself if no one else did"? (p. 16)

7. Why is sharecropping a slow way to build up a barn?

8. Give two examples of how Okonkwo tries to save his yams during the drought.

9. Why is the poor harvest like a sad funeral for the Igbo people?

10. What does Okonkwo learn through the drought and poor harvest?

Answers

1. Unoka is left to rot in the Evil Forest because the swelling in his stomach is an abomination to the Earth goddess.

2. Nwakibie has earned all but one title in Umuofia. He owns three huge barns, and he has nine wives and 30 children.

3. Nwakibie means that both he and Okonkwo are entitled to live well. If either of them denies the other prosperity, he should suffer.

4. The proverb means that a person does not run away from something without a reason.

5. Okonkwo is much like Obiako because his father is also unsuccessful.

6. Okonkwo is like the lizard in the proverb. He is praising himself since no one else will.

7. Sharecropping is a slow way to build up a barn because the farmer only reaps a third of the harvest for himself.

8. During the drought, Okonkwo tries to protect the yam seedlings from the sun by putting rings of sisal around them. He also prays for rain.

9. The livelihood of the Igbo people is dependent upon the yam. A good harvest means prosperity and life; a poor harvest is like death.

10. Okonkwo learns that he can survive any disaster.

Suggested Essay Topics

1. The author introduces Chika and one of Nwakibie's nine wives. He also mentions Okonkwo's mother and sisters. Based upon this information, describe at least three various roles women play in Igbo society. Use examples to support your points.

2. Explain the Igbo concept of *chi* and show how this concept relates to Okonkwo's desired success in life.

Chapter Four

New Characters:

Osugo: *a man who has taken no titles*

Ojiugo: *Okonkwo's youngest wife*

Ezeani: *Ani's priest*

Ogbuefi Ezeudu: *oldest man in the village*

Nwayieke: *old woman who lives near the udala tree*

Summary

Okonkwo is successful because he works hard. However, he is rude to unsuccessful men. For example, he calls Osugo a woman because he has not taken any titles. Okonkwo continues to rule his family with an iron hand. Ikemefuna, the hostage from Mbaino, has stayed with Okonkwo for three years. Nwoye's mother, Okonkwo's first wife, is kind to the boy and treats him as one of her own children. Ikemefuna gradually overcomes his fear and becomes inseparable from Nwoye. Okonkwo is fond of Ikemefuna, and the boy calls him father.

The ancestors know that crops will not grow without the blessing of Ani, the Great Earth Goddess. Therefore, before planting their crops, the Igbo observe a week in which no one says a harsh word and no work is done. During the Week of Peace, Ojiugo, Okonkwo's youngest wife, provokes him to a fiery rage. Ojiugo visits a friend who braids her hair; she does not return to cook the afternoon meal. Okonkwo forgets it is the Week of Peace and beats her.

Ezeani, Ani's priest, tells Okonkwo that he has committed a great evil. Ojiugo is wrong, but Okonkwo is wrong too. The crime he has committed could ruin the whole clan. Okonkwo has insulted the Earth goddess, and she could refuse to provide food. Ezeani commands Okonkwo to bring one female goat, one hen, a length of cloth, and 100 cowries to Ani. Okonkwo complies. Although Okonkwo is inwardly repentant, he will not admit his crime in public. The people say he has no respect for the clan, the gods, and the ancestors. Throughout the week the people talk about the *nso-ani*, or the crime that Okonkwo has committed. Ogbuefi Ezeudu, the oldest man in the village, says that the punishment for breaking the Week of Peace has become very mild.

After the Week of Peace, the people clear the bush to make new farms. Kites, or birds, appear from different directions. The people cultivate yams, which are a symbol of manliness and the king of the crops. The young plants are protected from the heat with rings of sisal leaves. When the heavier rains arrive, women plant maize, melons, and beans between the mounds of yams. The women weed

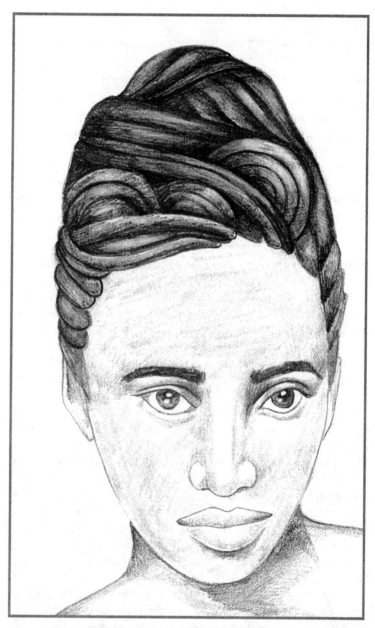

Ojiugo, Okonkwo's youngest wife, visits a friend who braids her hair.

the farms three times. When Nwoye and Ikemefuna try to prepare seed-yams, Okonkwo finds fault with their efforts and threatens them. Okonkwo particularly wants his eldest son, Nwoye, to be a great farmer and a great man.

Analysis

In Achebe's portrait of the Igbo people, daily life is controlled by religious forces. Although Okonkwo's *chi* may not be destined for greatness, his *chi* says "yes" to success because Okonkwo works so hard. The clan of Umuofia judges Okonkwo by the work of his hands; however, they also condemn Okonkwo's disrespect toward others.

The powerful Earth goddess, Ani, is a feminine force representing the spirit of fertility. As an agrarian society, the people of Umuofia depend upon their relationship with the Earth goddess. Yet, Okonkwo shows no fear of Ani. He commits a serious crime by beating his wife during the Week of Peace. This act reveals Okonkwo's impulsive and violent nature. His failure to observe the traditional peace is a foreshadowing of his failure to succeed in the traditional world in spite of his personal achievements. Okonkwo does not respect the feminine energy in the Igbo world, and he does not respect his wife. Although Okonkwo regrets his crime and makes amends, he cannot admit his mistake publicly because he is afraid of appearing weak like his father.

Okonkwo loses the balance of the masculine and feminine energies and is overcome by irrational, violent anger. He is also unable to show his affection for his adopted son, Ikemefuna, or his eldest son, Nwoye. In his desire to be strong and successful, Okonkwo is harsh to both Nwoye and Ikemefuna. He continues to stamp out the laziness he detects in Nwoye. Although Ikemefuna is beginning to feel comfortable in Okonkwo's homestead, he is identified as a sacrificial offering. The author clearly refers to the boy as a doomed, ill-fated lad given to Umuofia to atone for murder.

Study Questions

1. An old man refers to Okonkwo saying, "Looking at a king's mouth, one would think he never sucked at his mother's breast." (p. 19) What does he mean?

2. How does Okonkwo demonstrate his fondness for Ikemefuna?

3. Why does Nwoye's mother claim that Ojiugo has asked her to feed her children?

4. Why is Okonkwo's first wife always called "Nwoye's mother"?

5. What does the kola nut symbolize, and why does Ezeani refuse to accept it from Okonkwo during the Week of Peace?

6. Why do Okonkwo's enemies called him the little bird *nza*?

7. In the past, a man who broke the sacred peace was dragged around the village until he died. Why was the custom stopped?

8. In some clans, if a man dies during the Week of Peace, he is cast into the Evil Forest. He is not buried. What is the result of this action?

9. Compare and contrast the planting season with the month of harvest.

10. What does Nwoye mean when he decides that Nnadi lives in the land of Ikemefuna's favorite story?

Answers

1. The old man thinks it is incredible that Okonkwo, who has risen so suddenly from desperate poverty and misfortune and is now one of the lords of the clan, should forget his own humble origins and treat less successful men with disrespect.

2. When Okonkwo goes to feasts or meetings, he allows Ikemefuna to carry his stool and goatskin bag; this is traditionally a son's privilege.

3. Nwoye's mother minimizes Ojiugo's thoughtlessness and protects her.

4. Okonkwo's first wife is always called "Nwoye's mother" because she is honored as the mother of Okonkwo's heir, his first son.

5. The kola nut is a symbol of hospitality. Ezeani refuses to accept it because Okonkwo has offended Ani, the Earth goddess, by beating his wife during the Week of Peace.

6. Okonkwo's enemies called him the little bird *nza* because *nza* forgot who he was after a heavy meal and challenged his *chi*. Likewise, Okonkwo challenged the gods by violating the Peace of Ani.

7. The custom of dragging a man around the village was stopped because it spoiled the peace it was meant to preserve.

8. The dead who are thrown into the Evil Forest without burial become evil spirits who roam the earth and threaten the living.

9. The planting season and the month of harvest are periods of exact and hard work. The planting season is a serious time; the harvest is a light-hearted time.

10. Nnadi is just a character in a song; he is part of Ikemefuna's vivid imagination.

Suggested Essay Topics

1. Compare and contrast the way Okonkwo treats Osugo, his wives, and his sons. Is Okonkwo harsher to men, women, or children? Support your points with examples.

2. Discuss the symbolic meaning of the Week of Peace for the Igbo people. How does Okonkwo's anger violate the Week of Peace?

Chapter Five

New Characters:

Ekwefi: *Okonkwo's second wife*

Ezinma: *Okonkwo's daughter of his second wife; Ekwefi's only daughter*

Obiageli: *Okonkwo's daughter of his first wife; Nwoye's sister*

Nkechi: *Okonkwo's daughter of his third wife*

Summary

The Feast of the New Yam is a big event. It is held every year before the harvest to honor the ancestral spirits and Ani. Ani is the most important deity in Igbo cosmology because she is the source of all fertility. In addition to playing an active role in the daily lives of the people, she judges morality and conduct.

Okonkwo is edgy as his family prepares for the feast because he would rather be working in the farm. He accuses Ekwefi, his second wife, of killing a banana tree. He beats Ekwefi and leaves her crying with Ezinma, her only daughter. The beating serves as an outlet for Okonkwo's anger. Okonkwo picks up his rusty gun, and Ekwefi mutters something about guns that never shoot. Okonkwo hears the remark and pulls the trigger. His shot misses Ekwefi. Although the incident is upsetting, it does not dampen the spirit of the festival. The relatives of Okonkwo's wives arrive for the first day of feasting.

Wrestling matches between villages are held on the second day of the New Yam Festival. Ekwefi loves wrestling matches. Years ago, when she was the village beauty, Okonkwo won her heart by throwing the Cat in a wrestling match. Then, she ran away from her first husband to live with Okonkwo. Since then, Ekwefi has suffered much; she only has one daughter, whose name is Ezinma.

Obiageli, the daughter of Okonkwo's first wife, has been making *inyanga*, and she is showing off with her pot. She balances it on her head, folds her arms in front of her, and begins to sway like one of the women. When she breaks her pot, she laughs. However, as she gets closer to the homestead, Obiageli begins to cry. Ikemefuna signals the other children not to tattle on Obiageli.

The drums announce the wrestling matches and fill the air with excitement. Ezinma takes her father a dish to eat in his *obi*. Okonkwo is eating his first wife's meal. Obiageli sits waiting for her mother's empty bowl. Ezinma places her mother's dish before him and sits with Obiageli. Okonkwo is especially fond of Ezinma because she is a beauty like her mother. However, he only shows his fondness on rare occasions. Ezinma asks to carry her father's chair to the wrestling match. Okonkwo refuses. Nkechi, the daughter of Okonkwo's third wife, brings in his third and final dish of food.

Okonkwo takes a shot at Ekwefi, his second wife, during the Yam Festival.

Analysis

Like the Week of Peace, the Feast of the New Yam honors the ancestors and gods of the community. However, the feast presents another opportunity for Okonkwo to display his angry nature; he again offends the Earth goddess by taking a shot at his second wife, Ekwefi. Ekwefi is introduced as the wife who left her first husband because of her love of Okonkwo. Again, Okonkwo's actions disregard the feminine energy in Igbo society and result in violence. He is angry because he cannot work.

In this chapter, the author attempts to present a realistic portrait of a polygamous household, which is the key unit of agricultural production in Igbo society. In reality, many children are needed to plant, cultivate, and harvest crops; therefore, most men marry more than one wife. Historically, many wives enhanced a man's status and often increased the prestige of the first wife. The senior wife was the head of the household; she shared every title her husband acquired, and she managed her husband's younger wives. In many cases, the junior wives enjoyed security and prosperity in a large household. The Igbo women lived in their own houses, cooked for themselves, and raised their own children. In some cases women sold their crops in the marketplace and kept the proceeds. Igbo law also allowed an unhappy wife to leave her husband.

In this chapter, Ikemefuna is introduced as a sensitive youth who protects one of his sisters. It is significant that Ikemefuna stops the younger brothers from tattling on Obiageli because he is aware of what Okonkwo might do if he knows the truth. The girls in the family, Obiageli, Ezinma, and Nkechi, serve their father food in a specific order because they are the daughters of Okonkwo's first, second, and third wives. These girls are actually half-sisters. Okonkwo's first wife is never given a name. She is always called "Nwoye's mother" because she is identified with her eldest son. Ezinma seems to be a model daughter; however, she cannot carry her father's chair to the wrestling match because this is a boy's job. The Igbo culture clearly defines male and female roles. *Things Fall Apart* is fiction; nevertheless, this chapter provides a window on the daily lives of the Igbo people at a particular point in time and explains an important religious festival.

Study Questions

1. What is Ani's relationship with the ancestors?

2. Why are new yams offered to Ani and the ancestors at the festival?

3. Describe the New Yam Festival.

4. Does Ekwefi, Okonkwo's second wife, really kill the banana tree?

5. Nwoye's mother often calls Ezinma "Ezigbo." What does this name mean?

6. How does Okonkwo react when he hears the beating of the drums?

7. Why is Obiageli, Nwoye's sister, crying?

8. Why does Ikemefuna look at the other children sternly when Obiageli tells the adults the story about breaking her pot?

9. Why do Obiageli, Ezinma, and Nkechi serve their father food in this order?

10. Why can't Ezinma carry her father's chair to the wrestling match?

Answers

1. Ani is in close communion with the ancestors of the clan.

2. The people give honor and thanks to Ani and the ancestors by offering them new yams at the festival.

3. The New Yam Festival is a big event; the women scrub the walls of their houses and wash all the pots and bowls thoroughly. Wives and children decorate themselves; relatives are invited to the feast; and huge quantities of yam *foo-foo* and vegetable soup are prepared. The feast is held on the first day; the wrestling matches are held on the second day.

4. Ekwefi does not kill the banana tree. She simply removes some of the leaves to wrap food.

5. "Ezigbo" means "the good one."

6. The drums announcing the wrestling match fill Okonkwo with fire and the desire to conquer and subdue. He moves his feet to the beat of the drums.

7. Obiageli, Nwoye's sister, is crying because she broke her water pot.

8. Obiageli is acting sad in front of the adults. Ikemefuna does not want the other children to tattle on Obiageli.

9. The girls serve their father food in this order because Obiageli is the daughter of her father's first wife; Ezinma is the daughter of her father's second wife; and Nkechi is the daughter of her father's third wife.

10. Ezinma cannot carry her father's chair to the wrestling match because this is a boy's job. Men, women, boys, and girls play specific roles in the Igbo society.

Suggested Essay Topics

1. Okonkwo is angry because he is unable to work during the preparations for the New Yam Festival. Compare and contrast Okonkwo's behavior during the festival with his behavior during the Week of Peace.

2. Polygamy is defined as the practice of having more than one spouse at a time. The work and play of the women and children in this chapter provide examples of a harmonious polygamous household. Describe this household in terms of the relationships between Okonkwo's wives and children.

Chapter Six

New Characters:

Maduka: *the son of Obierika*

Chielo: *a priestess of Agbala*

Okafo: *a wrestler*

Ikezue: *a wrestler*

Summary

The whole village turns out for the wrestling match involving the nine villages of Umuofia. The drummers face the elders and a huge circle of spectators. There are seven drums arranged according to size in a long wooden basket. Three men beat the drums feverishly as if they are possessed by the spirits of the drums. Several young men keep order by beating the crowd back with palm branches. Finally, the two wrestling teams dance into the circle. The younger boys wrestle first, and the crowd roars as the third boy throws his opponent. Maduka, the son of Obierika, wins, and three young men from his team run forward and carry him on their shoulders through the cheering crowd.

Ekwefi and Chielo stand next to one another in the crowd. Chielo cannot believe that Ekwefi was nearly killed by Okonkwo. Chielo is an ordinary woman who also serves as the priestess of Agbala, the Oracle of the Hills and the Caves. She is very friendly with Ekwefi. She loves Ezinma and calls her "my daughter." It is hard to believe that this ordinary woman is the same person who prophesies when the spirit of the god Agbala is upon her.

Two teams with 12 men on each side wrestle. The last match is between the leaders of the teams. These men are the best wrestlers in all the nine villages. Okafo and Ikezue wrestle one another until the muscles on their arms, thighs, and backs stand out and twitch. It seems like an equal match, but Okafo uses a surprise maneuver and throws his opponent. Okafo is swept off his feet by his team and carried home as the villagers sing his praises.

Analysis

The wrestling match provides another example of life among the Igbo people. Achebe attempts to recreate the match of the New Yam Festival, which is one of the most exciting events in Igbo society. Historically, wrestling was an important sport among the Igbo because the matches allowed young men to gain recognition by demonstrating their strength and skill. The younger boys set the scene for the older, more experienced wrestlers. The match in this chapter reminds Okonkwo of his own accomplishments. The community involvement in the wrestling match illustrates the solidarity among the people in the nine-village consortium of Umuofia.

The drummers provide the beat and the background, and the drums serve as the pulse of the people. The excitement of the wrestling match, which involves the entire community, contrasts with the shadowy world of Chielo, the priestess of Agbala.

Chielo is introduced as an ordinary woman against the backdrop of the wrestling match. She is a friend of Ekwefi and Ezinma; however, she is also the priestess of Agbala, the Oracle of the Hills and the Caves. This is the same Oracle Unoka consulted about his poor harvests. Agbala is a minor god and a center of divination; the Oracle links the world of the living with the world of the dead. Historically, the Igbo people offered sacrifices, prayers, and invocations through the priest or priestess of the Oracle. Achebe implies that Chielo is not an ordinary person when she serves as Agbala's priestess.

Study Questions

1. Using context clues, define the Igbo word *ilo*.

2. Why is the ancient silk-cotton tree considered sacred?

3. Why do the young boys of 15 and 16 wrestle first?

4. Describe Chielo in ordinary life.

5. Give an example of Chielo's fondness for Ezinma.

6. What does Ekwefi mean when she says Ezinma is probably going to stay?

7. What is the most exciting moment in a wrestling match?

8. How do you know that Okafo and Ikezue are equally matched wrestlers?

9. What role do the drums play in the wrestling match?

10. Using context clues define the word *Amadiora*.

Answers

1. The Igbo word *ilo* refers to a playground or a large open area where meetings and sports events take place.

2. The ancient silk-cotton tree is considered sacred because the spirits of good children who are waiting to be born live there.

3. The young boys of 15 and 16 wrestle first in order to set the stage. They are actually practicing.

4. In ordinary life Chielo is a widow with two children. She is friendly with Ekwefi, and they share a common shed in the market.

5. Chielo shows her fondness for Ezinma by sending her bean cakes.

6. When Ekwefi says Ezinma is probably going to stay, she means she is probably going to live.

7. The most exciting moment in a wrestling match is when a man is thrown.

8. Okafo and Ikezue are equally matched because in the previous year, neither one threw the other. Both wrestlers have the same style, and they seem to know each other's moves beforehand.

9. The drums announce the wrestling match early in the day. The drums beat a rhythm of excitement. Like the crowd, the drums go mad when a wrestler is thrown. The drums are like the pulse of the nine villages.

10. *Amadiora* is the god of thunder and lightning.

Suggested Essay Topics

1. Describe Okonkwo's reaction to the wrestling match. Why do you think he reacts this way?

2. Describe the relationships among Chielo, Ekwefi, and Ezinma. How do you know that Chielo is really no ordinary person?

Chapter Seven

Summary

The elders seemed to have forgotten about Ikemefuna, who has been living in Okonkwo's household for three years. Ikemefuna is a positive influence on Nwoye. He is described as a yam tendril in the rainy season. Ikemefuna and Nwoye listen to Okonkwo's stories about war and violence. Nwoye remembers the stories his mother used to tell of the tortoise, the bird *eneke-nti-oba*, and the quarrel between Earth and Sky. Nwoye knows his father wants him to be a man, so he pretends he does not like women's stories.

Ogbuefi Ezeudu, the oldest man in the village tells Okonkwo that Umuofia has decided to kill Ikemefuna because the Oracle of Hills and Caves has pronounced the boy's death. However, Ezeudu cautions Okonkwo saying, ". . . I want you to have nothing to do with it. He calls you father." (p. 40) When the elders gather, Okonkwo tells Ikemefuna he is going home. Nwoye cries, and Okonkwo beats him severely. Ikemefuna is confused because his old home has grown distant.

The men of Umuofia travel down a narrow footpath through the heart of the forest. Ikemefuna carries a pot of palm wine on his head and walks in their midst. He feels uneasy at first, but he is reassured because Okonkwo walks behind him. Ikemefuna feels as though Okonkwo is his father. He was never fond of his real father. Ikemefuna remembers his mother and his younger sister, and he wonders if his mother is still alive.

One of the men clears his throat and growls at Ikemefuna. It sends a cold shiver of fear down the boy's back. Okonkwo has withdrawn to the rear of the party. Ikemefuna feels his legs give way under him. The man raises his machete, and Okonkwo looks away. He hears the blow. Ikemefuna's pot falls and breaks. Ikemefuna cries, "My father, they have killed me!" (p. 43) Ikemefuna runs toward Okonkwo. Dazed with fear, Okonkwo draws his machete and kills Ikemefuna.

Nwoye knows that Ikemefuna has been killed. Something has snapped inside him, and he feels limp. He had the same feeling

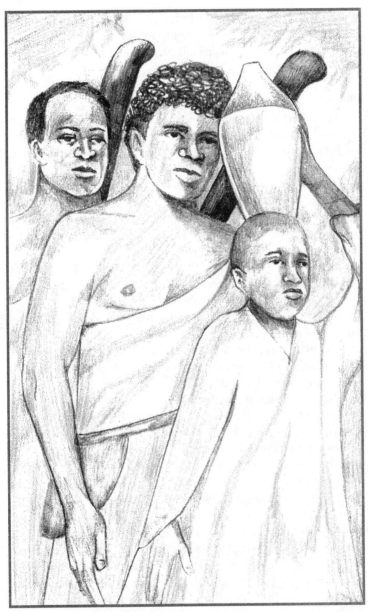

The fearful Ikemefuna is reassured on the journey through the forest because Okonkwo is walking behind him.

during the harvest season when he heard infants crying in the bush. Nwoye has heard that twins are put in earthenware pots and thrown away in the Evil Forest. A deep chill overcomes him when Okonkwo returns after killing Ikemefuna.

Analysis

Ikemefuna is compared to a yam tendril in the rainy season because he is full of the sap of new life. Although Okonkwo does not display his emotions publicly, he loves his adopted son Ikemefuna. This is evident because Ikemefuna carries his stool and calls Okonkwo father. Ezeudu, the eldest man in the village, a leader, and an authority figure, explains the Oracle's command to kill Ikemefuna. Neither Ezeudu nor the Oracle give any reason for requiring Ikemefuna's death. However, Ezeudu clearly tells Okonkwo not to take part in the ritual killing.

Okonkwo does not listen to Ezeudu's warning. He joins the party, and he provides comfort and assurance for his unsuspecting adopted son on the journey through the forest. However, Okonkwo does retire to the rear of the party when Ikemefuna receives the first blow. He does not expect the injured boy to run to him. Okonkwo deals the death blow to Ikemefuna as part of a ritual sacrifice because he is afraid of appearing weak. Ikemefuna's journey is reminiscent of the biblical story of Abraham and Isaac. However, here, no animal is substituted for Ikemefuna as a ram is substituted for Isaac. The incident may be Achebe's attempt to address ritual sacrifice in Christian terms. In any event, Okonkwo kills Ikemefuna, a skillful hunter and sensitive musician. Ikemefuna has achieved the balance of the masculine and feminine energies in Igbo society that escapes Okonkwo. Okonkwo's ritual killing of this balance may represent his own self-destruction.

Okonkwo loves Ikemefuna, yet he kills him; Okonkwo also loves Nwoye, yet he devastates his son by killing Ikemefuna. Nwoye is haunted by other unexplained deaths. The Igbo believe that twins are abnormal and leave the infants to die in the bush; otherwise, the entire community might suffer. The cries of infants abandoned in the forest and the ritual killing of Ikemefuna chill Nwoye's spirit. Nwoye is sensitive, and he does not understand these customs.

Study Questions

1. Why is Ikemefuna compared to a yam tendril in the rainy season?

2. What are some of the difficult masculine tasks Nwoye enjoys doing?

3. Why would Nwoye pretend to be annoyed and grumble about women?

4. How does Okonkwo feel when he hears Nwoye grumbling about women?

5. Even though Nwoye knows it is right to be masculine, he still prefers the stories that his mother tells. Why?

6. Explain the story of the bird *eneke-nti-oba*.

7. Why are the people of Umuofia so excited about the locusts?

8. Describe some of the chores the men and women do after the harvest.

9. What does Ikemefuna remember when the men speak in low tones?

10. Why do the women walk quickly when they hear abandoned infants crying in the forest?

Answers

1. Ikemefuna is like a yam tendril in the rainy season because he is full of the sap of new life.

2. Some of the difficult masculine tasks Nwoye enjoys doing around the homestead include splitting wood and pounding food.

3. Nwoye grumbles about women in order to appear more masculine.

4. Okonkwo is happy when he hears Nwoye grumbling about women.

5. Nwoye prefers his mother's stories because Okonkwo's masculine stories are about violence and bloodshed. Nwoye is a sensitive youth.

6. The bird *eneke-nti-oba* challenged the whole world to a wrestling contest and was thrown by the Cat.

7. The locusts descend once in a generation and reappear every year for seven years. Then they disappear for another lifetime. Everyone wants the locusts to camp in Umuofia for the night because they are good to eat.

8. After the harvest, Okonkwo, Nwoye, and Ikemefuna repair the walls of the compound while the women collect firewood.

9. When Ikemefuna hears the men speaking in low tones, he remembers leaving his first home as a hostage.

10. The women walk quickly when they hear abandoned infants crying in the forest because, like Nwoye, they are disconcerted by this Igbo custom.

Suggested Essay Topics

1. Okonkwo is inwardly pleased with his son Nwoye. He attributes Nwoye's development to Ikemefuna. Why does Okonkwo want Nwoye to be a prosperous man and feed the ancestors with regular sacrifices?

2. Okonkwo loves Ikemefuna, and the boy calls him father. Yet, Okonkwo kills his adopted son in cold blood. Why does Okonkwo kill Ikemefuna? Ezeudu is an elder and a leader in the community. Why didn't Okonkwo heed Ezeudu's advice? Is Okonkwo making up his own rules, regulations, and customs? Prove your points.

Chapter Eight

New Characters:

Obierika: *Okonkwo's friend and confidant*

Ofoedu: *a villager who comes with a message*

Ogbuefi Ndulue: *the oldest man in Ire*

Ozoemena: *Ogbuefi Ndulue's first wife*

Akueke: *Obierika's daughter*

Obidrika: *a brother of Obierika*

Machi: *the eldest brother of Obierika*

Dimaragana: *a man who would not lend his knife for cutting up a dog*

Umezulike: *a man who taps Okonkwo's palm trees*

Ibe: *a young suitor of Akueke*

Ukegbu: *the father of Ibe*

Amadi: *a leper who often passes by Obierika's compound*

Summary

Okonkwo does not eat for two days after Ikemefuna's death; he drinks palm wine day and night. He cannot forget Ikemefuna, and he admonishes himself for becoming a shivering old woman. Okonkwo visits his friend Obierika and asks him why he refused to kill Ikemefuna. He asks Obierika if he questions the authority of the Oracle who said that the boy must die. Obierika explains that he is not afraid of blood, but the Oracle did not ask him specifically to carry out its decision. Obierika says that if he had been Okonkwo, he would have stayed at home. Okonkwo's action will not please the Earth goddess; it is the kind of thing for which she wipes out whole families. Obierika says that if the Oracle declared that his own son should be killed, he would neither dispute the decree nor help carry out the ritual murder.

Ofoedu, a villager, arrives with a message. He says that Ogbuefi Ndulue, the oldest man in Ire, has died. It is very strange. Ozoemena, Ndulue's first wife, has died on the same day. It was always said that Ndulue and Ozoemena had one mind. He could not do anything without telling her. Ogbuefi Ndulue was a strong man in his youth and led Umuofia to war. Okonkwo does not understand why a strong man would share his thoughts with his wife. The men also talk about Umezulike, the man who taps Okonkwo's palm trees. Obierika says that sometimes he regrets taking the *ozo* title because

The men of Umuofia talk about customs and marriage arrangements.

men of this title cannot climb tall trees; they can only tap short trees while standing on the ground. Okonkwo argues that it is good that the *ozo* title is esteemed. In other clans, like Abame and Aninta, the *ozo* title is worth very little. Obierika recants and says that he is just joking.

Then Ibe arrives with his father, Ukegbu, and his uncle. Ibe wants to marry Obierika's beautiful daughter, Akueke. Obierika and his brothers negotiate Akueke's bride-price. Obidrika, Obierika's brother, presents a bundle of 30 short broomsticks to Ukegbu. Ukegbu consults his family and returns 15 sticks to Obierika. Machi, Obierika's eldest brother, claims that they do not want to go below 30. He adds 10 sticks to the 15 and returns the bundle to Ukegbu. Akueke's bride-price is finally settled at 20 bags of cowries. Obierika's wives and his son, Maduka, serve food and palm wine.

Later, the men eat and drink and criticize the customs of their neighbors. In Abame and Aninta men haggle over a bride-price; they climb trees and pound *foo-foo* for their wives. Their customs are upside-down. Obierika's eldest brother says, "But what is good in one place is bad in another place." (p. 51) In some areas a suitor offers bags of cowries until his in-laws say stop. Okonkwo heard that in some places a man's children belong to his wife's family. Obierika says there was a story of white men, the color of chalk. The only white man they know is Amadi, a leper who passes by Obierika's compound.

Analysis

It is the season of rest. Okonkwo is a man of action and not thought; he is frustrated because he cannot work, and he is haunted by the murder of Ikemefuna. Obierika chastises Okonkwo and questions the morality of his participation in the ritual sacrifice. He says he would have respected the Oracle, but he would not have participated in killing his own son. Obierika is more balanced than Okonkwo because he understands how to temper the rules and regulations of the traditional Igbo religion. Obierika is like Ezeudu who warned Okonkwo not to kill his son. Obierika will provide insight throughout the rest of the novel; he may serve as the author's mouthpiece.

Okonkwo is also worried about Nwoye, who seems weak like his grandfather Unoka. Whenever Okonkwo thinks about his father's weakness and failure, he thinks about his own strength and success. Okonkwo continues to juxtapose his own achievements with the inadequacies of his father and son. In Okonkwo's mind, a weak man is like a woman. Therefore, Okonkwo cannot understand why a strong man like Ogbuefi Ndulue has shared his thoughts with Ozoemena, his first wife, throughout his life. This elderly couple died as they had lived—together. They are a symbol of the balance of the masculine and feminine energies in life. It is this balance that Okonkwo cannot achieve. The dual death of Ndulue and Ozoemena clearly identifies this moral code for Okonkwo; his inability to understand the code dramatizes the discrepancy between his understanding and the values of the clan as a whole.

The conversation about the palm wine tappers provides some comic relief and allows Obierika to question Igbo customs. At the same time, the bride-price negotiations provide another backdrop illustrating Igbo life. In Igbo society, discussions leading to marriage involve the extended family, and serious negotiations are necessary because every adult is responsible for building a family and strengthening the lineage. Because a woman leaves her homestead when she marries, her family receives a bride-price to compensate for their loss. In the discussion about customs, Obierika again questions assumptions about culture. The men are aware that customs in one area are not accepted in another. Even Okonkwo realizes that the world is wide. However, the final passage is an ironic foreshadowing. The Igbo laugh about the white man; they are certainly not worried about pale men the color of chalk.

Study Questions

1. What does Okonkwo mean when he says a bowl of pounded yams can throw Nwoye in a wrestling match?

2. What does Okonkwo mean when he says, "Where are the young suckers that will grow when the old banana tree dies?" (p. 46)

3. Why would Okonkwo have been happier if Ezinma had been a boy?

4. Okonkwo springs to his feet to visit his friend Obierika. What does this image reveal about Okonkwo?

5. What is the meaning of the proverb "A child's fingers are not scalded by a piece of hot yam which its mother puts into its palm". (p. 47)

6. Explain Okonkwo's reaction to the deaths of Ogbuefi Ndulue and Ozoemena and the idea that they had "one mind." What does this reaction reveal about Okonkwo's understanding of the feminine principle?

7. Why does Obierika think Maduka is too sharp?

8. What is the meaning of the proverb "When mother-cow is chewing grass its young ones watch its mouth"? (p. 49)

9. Why does Akueke's mother say that waist beads and fire are not friends?

10. What is Akueke's bride-price, and how do the men arrive at the price?

Answers

1. Nwoye is not a powerful or skillful wrestler.

2. Okonkwo wonders who will follow in his footsteps. His children do not seem to resemble him.

3. Ezinma has the right spirit.

4. Okonkwo is a man of action.

5. The proverb means that a mother will never hurt her child. Likewise, Okonkwo believes the Earth goddess will not punish him for obeying her.

6. Okonkwo feels that the simultaneous deaths of Ogbuefi Ndulue and Ozoemena are very strange. He cannot believe that Ndulue and his wife had "one mind." He thought Ndulue was a strong man. This reaction reveals that Okonkwo does not understand the nature, function, and power of the feminine principle in Igbo cosmology.

7. Maduka is always in a hurry; he often does not listen to the whole message.

8. The proverb means that children imitate their parents. Likewise, Maduka has been watching Obierika and imitating him.

9. She fears that some day Akueke's waist beads will catch on fire while she is cooking.

10. Akueke's bride-price is finally settled at 20 bags of cowries. The men negotiate with the bundles of sticks.

Suggested Essay Topics

1. Compare and contrast Okonkwo and his friend Obierika. Which one of the men is more balanced? Prove your position with a good example.

2. Discuss the role of women in founding and maintaining a family in Igbo society. Explain the custom of the bride-price.

Chapter Nine

New Character:

Okagbue Uyanwa: *a famous medicine man*

Summary

Okonkwo finally sleeps. He questions his uneasiness about killing Ikemefuna. As a mosquito buzzes in his ear, he remembers a story his mother used to tell him. When Mosquito asked Ear to marry him, she fell on the floor laughing. Ear thought Mosquito looked like a skeleton and insinuated that he would not live much longer. Mosquito was humiliated. To this day, any time Mosquito passes by, he tells Ear that he is still alive. Later in the chapter, Ekwefi tells Ezinma another story. The snake-lizard gave his mother seven baskets of raw vegetables to cook; they yielded three baskets of cooked vegetables. As a result, the snake-lizard killed his mother. Then, he brought another seven baskets of raw vegetables and cooked them himself; again they yielded three baskets of cooked vegetables. The snake-lizard was distraught, so he killed himself.

During the night, Ekwefi, Okonkwo's second wife, tells him that Ezinma is dying. She is shivering on a mat beside a huge fire. Okonkwo collects bark, leaves, and grass to make a medicine to cure her fever, or *iba*. Ezinma is her mother's only child and the center of her world. Their relationship is a companionship of equals. Ekwefi has suffered; she has borne 10 children, but nine of them died in infancy, after which, she sank into despair and resignation. After the second child died, a diviner told Okonkwo it was an *ogbanje*, or a changeling child who dies and returns to its mother's womb to be reborn. Okonkwo called in another diviner, Okagbue Uyanwa, who was a medicine man famous for his knowledge of *ogbanje* children. When Ekwefi's third child died, he mutilated the body with a razor and dragged it into the Evil Forest so it would never return.

Ekwefi loves Ezinma, but everyone knows she is an *ogbanje*. Ekwefi believes Ezinma is going to stay on Earth because a medicine man had dug up her *iyi-uwa*, or the sacred stone that linked her to the spirit world. He had asked Ezinma where the stone was buried, and she led him through the bush. Finally, she pointed to a spot in the homestead. Okonkwo and the medicine man had dug a huge pit and found the *iyi-uwa*. Since then, Ezinma had not been sick.

Okonkwo's other wives say Ezinma has a fever, but Ekwefi does not hear them. Okonkwo prepares the medicine, and Ekwefi tends the medicine pot. He brings a low stool and a thick mat. Ezinma sits on the stool next to the steaming pot, and Okonkwo throws a thick mat over her head. She struggles to escape from the overpowering steam, but she is held down. Finally, she emerges drenched in perspiration. Ekwefi dries her off, and Ezinma sleeps.

Analysis

The stories about the mosquito and the snake-lizard provide comic relief and a backdrop of daily life in the homestead during the intense story about Ezinma. Mosquito was humiliated by Ear, so he buzzes every time he gets close to her. The snake-lizard also explains daily life when he learns what happens to cooked

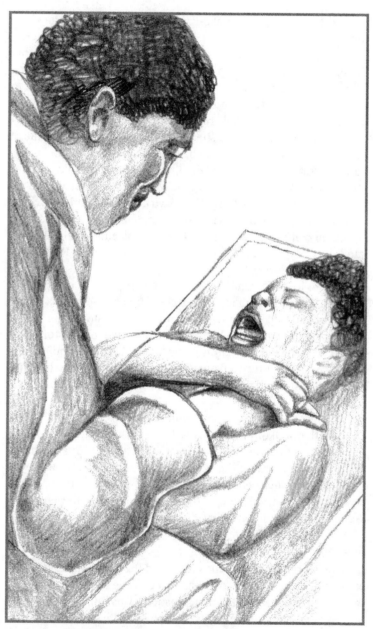

Okonkwo prepares a medicine to cure Ezinma's fever.

vegetables. However, both stories also explain relationships that are out of balance. The feminine Ear rejects the masculine Mosquito. The snake-lizard is completely off balance and commits murder and suicide over cooked vegetables. Perhaps the snake-lizard killed himself because he unjustly murdered his mother. These stories may provide parallels to Okonkwo's gender imbalance.

The religious concept of *ogbanje* is also illustrated in this chapter. An *ogbanje* is a child who dies and then reenters its mother's womb to be born again. The constant birth and death of the child torments its unfortunate parents. The concept is an example of a religious belief that explains natural phenomena. The *iyi-uwa* is a symbol of the child's link with the spirit world. By digging up this smooth pebble wrapped in a dirty rag, the medicine man breaks Ezinma's bond with the world of the *ogbanje*. His quiet, patient voice lends calm to the scene, but also contrasts with the intensity of his mission. This chapter also shows Okonkwo as both a loving and angry father. He cares for Ezinma by collecting materials to make her medicine, but he also threatens her if she does not locate her *iyi-uwa*.

Study Questions

1. Describe the story Okonkwo's mother used to tell him that explained why mosquitoes buzz in people's ears.

2. Give two examples proving that the relationship between Ezinma and Ekwefi was a companionship of equals.

3. Why did Ekwefi stay with her people during her third pregnancy?

4. How was Ekwefi's despair reflected in the names she gave her children?

5. Describe the medicine man famous for his knowledge of *ogbanje* children.

6. Why did the medicine man drag the corpse of the dead *ogbanje* child into the Evil Forest?

7. Why did Ekwefi grow bitter about her own *chi*?

8. Why did Ezinma take the medicine man and her family through the bush and back to the homestead in order to find the *iyi-uwa*?

9. As Ezinma and Ekwefi are cooking yams, they discuss the fact that large quantities of vegetables cook down to smaller quantities by telling the story of the snake-lizard. Why did the snake-lizard kill his mother and himself?

10. Why does Okonkwo tell Ekwefi to watch the medicine pot carefully?

Answers

1. When Mosquito asked Ear to marry him, she fell on the floor laughing. Ear thought Mosquito looked like a skeleton and insinuated that he would not live much longer. Mosquito was humiliated, so any time he passes by, he tells Ear that he is still alive.

2. Ezinma does not call her mother *Nne* like other children. She calls her by her name. They share secrets like eating eggs together.

3. The medicine man said Ekwefi would trick the wicked *ogbanje* and break the cycle of birth and death if she stayed with her people during her pregnancy.

4. Ekwefi's despair was reflected in the following names she gave her children: Onwumbiko "Death I implore you;" Ozoemena "May it not happen again;" and Onwuma "Death may please himself."

5. The medicine man was striking. He was very tall; he had a full beard and a bald head. He was light in complexion, and his eyes were fiery.

6. The medicine man dragged the dead child into the Evil Forest because then the *ogbanje* would think twice about entering its mother's womb and coming to life again.

7. Ekwefi wishes her co-wives well, but she has grown bitter. She feels that it is her evil *chi* that denies her good fortune.

Ekwefi's bitterness does not flow outward to others but inward into her own soul.

8. Ezinma was looking for the *iyi-uwa* herself as she took everyone on a journey through the bush and then back to her own homestead.

9. The snake-lizard gave his mother seven baskets of raw vegetables to cook. When they yielded only three baskets of cooked vegetables, he killed her. Then, he brought another seven baskets of raw vegetables and cooked them himself; again they yielded three baskets of cooked vegetables. The snake-lizard then killed himself. He may have been upset about the vegetables, or he may have realized he murdered his mother unjustly.

10. Okonkwo tells Ekwefi to watch the medicine pot carefully because if the medicine boils over, its power will evaporate.

Suggested Essay Topics

1. The concept of *ogbanje* is foreign to Western readers. Explain the concept, and show how Ekwefi's sorrow contributes to her love for Ezinma.

2. Okonkwo shows a softer, more loving side in his relationship with Ezinma. Provide two examples from this chapter illustrating Okonkwo's care and concern.

Chapter Ten

New Characters:

Mgbafo: *a woman who is beaten by her husband*

Odukwe: *Mgbafo's eldest brother*

Uzowulu: *Mgbafo's husband*

Summary

Trials are held in the center of Umuofia. Only the men participate; the women observe as outsiders. The titled elders sit on stools,
and a powerful gong sounds. The people hear the terrifying, gut-
tural voices of the *egwugwu*, or the nine masked spirits of the clan.
Each *egwugwu* represents one of the villages in Umuofia. The leader
is named Evil Forest; he is the eldest *egwugwu*, and smoke pours
out of his head. All the other *egwugwu* sit in order of seniority after
him. He looks terrible. His body is made of smoked raffia, and his
huge wooden face is painted white except for his round hollow eyes
and large charred teeth. He has two powerful horns on the top of
his head.

Uzowulu is a wife-beater who put his case before the spirits of
the ancestors. He has married Mgbafo properly and offered money
and yams as bride-price. He does not owe his in-laws anything,
yet they beat him and took away his wife and children. He wants
his wife back, or he wants the bride-price returned. Mgbafo's brothers refuse. Odukwe, Mgbafo's brother, confirms the story. He says
Uzowulu is a beast because he has beaten Mgbafo every day for
nine years. He beat her when she was pregnant, and he beat her
when she was ill. The brothers agree that the children belong to
Uzowulu, but they are too young to leave their mother. They say
Mgbafo will return if Uzowulu recovers from his madness; however, if he beats Mgbafo again, they will cut off his genitals.

The nine *egwugwu* confer in their house. The metal gong and
the flute sound. Evil Forest settles the dispute. He tells Uzowulu to
go to his in-laws with a pot of wine and beg his wife to return. He
says it is not bravery when a man fights a woman. Evil Forest tells
Odukwe that if Uzowulu supplies wine, Mgbafo should return with
him. One elder wonders why such a trifle is put before the
egwugwu. The people say that Uzowulu will not listen to any other
decision. Then two other groups present a great land case to the
egwugwu.

Analysis

This chapter introduces and defines the concept of *egwugwu*.
The *egwugwu* are elders who wear masks and dress as ancestors.
They represent the spirits of the ancestors and speak in a strange

The *egwugwu* are masked men, or elders in the community, who represent the ancestors.

gutteral language. When the *egwugwu* appear, the women and children scream and run away. The trial attempts to represent the judicial system among the Igbo people. The masked spirits of the
ancestors judge civil and criminal disputes and serve as a center
of political power. The decision of the *egwugwu* reflects the moral
code of the people of Umuofia. Although the *egwugwu* are a secret
society of men impersonating spirits, they are understood as sacred spirits by the people. It is necessary to understand the role of
the *egwugwu* in order to comprehend the conflict and resolution
of the plot of *Things Fall Apart.*

   The trial of Uzowulu clearly identifies wife-beating as deviant
behavior in the Igbo moral code. The decision denouncing
Uzowulu also provides a clear judgment on Okonkwo's violent attacks on his wives. Okonkwo is a paradox. He seems to esteem Igbo
values since he is working so hard to succeed in Igbo society, yet
he himself beats his wives. Okonkwo's wives and the reader notice
that the second *egwugwu* has a springy walk and that Okonkwo is
not among the men in the audience. The second *egwugwu* is
Okonkwo; therefore, Okonkwo himself sits in judgment against
wife-beating.

   In his recreation of Igbo life, Achebe does not emphasize the
political role of women. In the traditional Igbo world, women not
only regulated markets, but they also settled civil and marital disputes. In this chapter, the male *egwugwu* are the authority figures
who settle the case against Uzowulu. However, historically, Igbo
women would have shamed the wife-beater by "sitting" on him or
singing rude songs and making obscene gestures. Many critics feel
the omission of female authority in Igbo society is a weakness in
Things Fall Apart. The reader encounters women who cook, braid
their hair, and run away from *egwugwu.* Female characters are not
portrayed as powerful market women or judges. Some critics feel
that a balanced portrayal of women and their roles in Igbo society
would be more realistic and historically accurate.

Study Questions

   1. Why does Evil Forest address Uzowulu saying, "Uzowulu's
       body, I salute you"? (p. 64)

2. Why does Evil Forest say, "Uzowulu's body, do you know me?" (p. 64)

3. What is the law of Umuofia concerning the bride-price of a woman who runs away from her husband?

4. How does Evil Forest keep order when the crowd roars with laughter during the trial?

5. What role do Uzowulu's neighbors play in the trial?

6. Why do Evil Forest and the other *egwugwu* run a few steps in the direction of the women?

7. What are some of the names Evil Forest gives himself?

8. What is the purpose of the metal gong, the drums, and the flute?

9. Why will Uzowulu listen to the decision of the *egwugwu*?

10. The *egwugwu* hear a land case after Uzowulu's case. What is a land case?

Answers

1. Spirits always address humans as bodies.

2. Evil Forest asks Uzowulu if he recognizes him as one of the living. Uzowulu responds, "How can I know you father? You are beyond our knowledge." (p. 64) Evil Forest emphasizes the point that he is not one of the living.

3. The law of Umuofia says that if a woman runs away from her husband, the bride-price must be returned.

4. Evil Forest keeps order when the crowd roars with laughter during the trial by rising to his feet. A steady cloud of smoke rises from his head.

5. The neighbors testify that Uzowulu beat his wife.

6. The women flee in terror, but they return to their places almost immediately. The *egwugwu* instill fear in the women.

7. Evil Forest calls himself "Dry-meat-that-fills-the-mouth," and "Fire-that-burns-without-faggots." A faggot is a dry stick. (p. 66)

8. The metal gong, the drums, and the flute all contribute to the excitement of the trial in the presence of the *egwugwu*. The instruments announce different sections of the trial.

9. Uzowulu will listen to the decision of the *egwugwu* because they represent the ancestral spirits.

10. A land case is a dispute over property.

Suggested Essay Topics

1. Explain the judicial function of the *egwugwu* and the relationship of the *egwugwu* to the living. Note the relationship of the *egwugwu* to Igbo women.

2. How do you know that Okonkwo is one of the *egwugwu*? What qualifications does Okonkwo have to enter the secret society? Support your points with examples.

Chapter Eleven

New Characters:

Nwayieke: *woman who is notorious for her late cooking*

Anene: *Ekwefi's first husband*

Summary

Ekwefi tells Ezinma a story about the Tortoise. It was a time of famine, and all the birds were invited to a feast in the sky. Tortoise, a great orator, convinced the birds to take him along. He told them to select new names for the feast. Tortoise took the name "All of you." The men in the sky thought Tortoise was the king of the birds and declared they had prepared the feast for "all of you." Since that was Tortoise's new name, he ate the best portions of food and drank two pots of palm wine. The birds ate the leftovers. They were very angry and left Tortoise in the sky without wings to fly. Tortoise sent a message with Parrot asking his wife to put soft things around his homestead so he could jump down from the sky without danger.

However, Parrot was very angry; he told Tortoise's wife to put hard things around the homestead. When Tortoise jumped from the sky, he crashed. He did not die, but his shell broke into pieces and a great medicine man had to mend his shell. This story explains why the Tortoise has a bumpy and cracked shell.

The night is very dark, and Ekwefi and Ezinma hear the high-pitched voice of Chielo, the priestess of Agbala, prophesying. She says Agbala wants to see Ezinma in the hills and caves. Chielo carries Ezinma on her back. Ekwefi follows Chielo, but she cannot see anything in the darkness. As Ekwefi runs after the priestess, it seems as if Chielo is running too. Then Chielo stops. She is only a few feet ahead of Ekwefi. Ekwefi is terrified, and Chielo screams. Ekwefi lets Chielo increase the distance between them. They travel all the way to the farthest village in the clan. Then, Chielo turns around. It is a long journey. Ekwefi is afraid Chielo might see her as the day dawns. She is numb like a sleepwalker. Finally, Chielo heads for the hills. She and Ezinma enter a cave through a tiny hole. Ekwefi waits, and Okonkwo appears behind her. As they stand there together, Ekwefi remembers how she had married her first husband, Anene, because Okonkwo was too poor to marry. Then two years later, she ran away to marry Okonkwo. She is grateful for his support at the end of this haunting journey.

Analysis

On the surface, the story of Tortoise explains why the turtle's shell is cracked. Traditional folklore again explains natural phenomena, and storytelling illustrates the close relationship between Ezinma and her mother. However, the animal fable may send a political message, and the story may be understood as an allegory of resistance. Tortoise is like a colonial power, and the birds are like colonized people. Tortoise uses language to deceive the birds. Parrot uses language to deceive Tortoise. The conflict is resolved when Tortoise falls upon his own weapons. Perhaps the author is indicating that both language and arms are necessary for oppressed people to resist domination.

It is against this backdrop of storytelling that Chielo transports Ezinma to the god Agbala, who is the Oracle of the Hills and Caves. Chielo speaks in a shrill, high-pitched voice, and she has

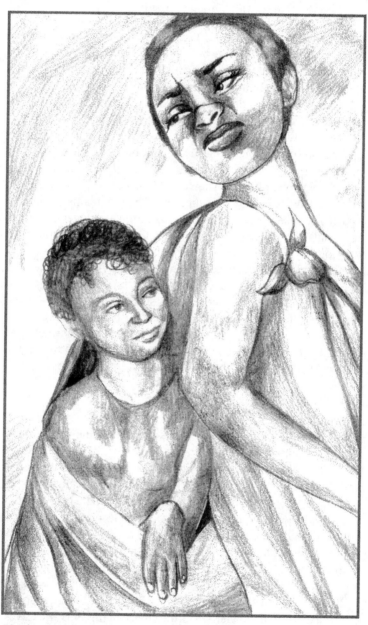

Chielo, the priestess of the god Agbala, carries Ezinma on her back to the oracle of the hills and caves.

superhuman strength as she carries Ezinma all night long throughout the nine villages and then back to the hills and caves. Chielo is
possessed by the spirit of Agbala, and she is completely different
from the ordinary woman she was in the marketplace. Chielo cannot provide the human sympathy, compassion, and companionship Ekwefi needs on the journey because she is devoid of
humanity in this situation. In contrast, Okonkwo emerges as a
humble husband and father in this chapter. Okonkwo does not
challenge the Oracle; he simply supports his wife and daughter.
The encounter emphasizes the relationship between the spirit
world and the world of the living. The night's experience also gives
Ekwefi an opportunity to reminisce about her youth and her love
for Okonkwo.

Study Questions

1. Why don't the birds want Tortoise to join them at the feast in the sky?

2. How does Tortoise convince the birds to allow him to join them at the feast?

3. How is Tortoise able to fly with the birds of the sky?

4. What are some of the hard things Tortoise's wife takes out of the house to prepare for Tortoise's fall?

5. Why does Ezinma cry when Chielo calls her "my daughter"?

6. Why does Ekwefi recoil from Chielo when she turns around?

7. Why does Ekwefi doubt the wisdom of her coming to the hills and caves?

8. How could a woman like Chielo carry a child the size of Ezinma for such a long distance?

9. How does Ekwefi know they have reached the ring of hills?

10. Who joins Ekwefi as she waits for Chielo and Ezinma?

Answers

1. The birds do not want Tortoise to join them at the feast in the sky because it is a time of famine. Tortoise is cunning and ungrateful.

2. Tortoise convinces the birds to allow him to join them by explaining that he is a changed man. Tortoise has a sweet tongue, and he is a great orator.

3. Tortoise is able to fly because the birds give him feathers to make wings.

4. Tortoise's wife takes out hard things like hoes, machetes, spears, guns, and a cannon to prepare for Tortoise's fall.

5. Ezinma cries because Chielo's voice is different and everything seems strange.

6. Ekwefi needs human companionship and sympathy. However, Chielo is possessed; she is a different woman than she was in the marketplace.

7. Ekwefi doubts the wisdom of her coming to the hills and caves because she is powerless and she would not dare enter the underground caves.

8. It would take a miracle for a woman like Chielo to carry a child the size of Ezinma for such a long distance. On this night Chielo is not an ordinary woman; she is a priestess possessed by the spirit of Agbala.

9. As soon as Chielo steps into this ring, her voice doubles in strength and is thrown back on all sides.

10. Okonkwo joins Ekwefi as she waits for the priestess and her daughter.

Suggested Essay Topics

1. Explain how the story of Tortoise and the birds fits in with some of the other stories Achebe has told about animals throughout the novel. Explain the purpose of these stories.

2. Explain the Oracle and Chielo's relationship with her god. Explain why all the characters, Okonkwo, Ekwefi, Ezinma, and Chielo, were powerless to alter the events of this dark night.

Chapter Twelve

New Characters:

Nwankwo: *a man in Obierika's household who is sent to buy a goat*

Mgbogo: *a woman who is home with a fever*

Udenkwo: *a woman who is home with her infant*

Ezelagbo: *a woman whose husband's cow is let loose*

Summary

Okonkwo has not slept during the night because he is worried and anxious. However, he does not show his feelings. He has gone to the shrine, but he realizes that Chielo has traveled through the nine villages. He waits at home and returns to the shrine four times. Finally, he finds Ekwefi. While he waits with her, Chielo crawls out of the shrine on her belly like a snake. Ezinma is sleeping on her back. The priestess does not look at Okonkwo or Ekwefi. She returns to the compound and silently places Ezinma on her bed.

The next day Obierika, Okonkwo's friend, celebrates his daughter's *uri*, or betrothal. This ceremony marks the payment of the bride-price. Ibe, the suitor, brings palm wine to the *umuada*, or the gathering of the daughters in the family. The central figures are the bride and her mother, but many other women help cook for the whole village. Chielo, the priestess, participates like an ordinary woman. However, as the feast is being prepared, a cow escapes from its corral. Five women stay behind with the cooking pots, while the other women chase the cow back to its owner. The women charge the owner of the cow with a heavy fine. They also identify the women who have not participated in this social action as they are required. Mgbogo is ill, and Udenkwo has just given birth, so they are excused.

Obierika's in-laws arrive carrying 50 pots of palm wine. Then Ibe, the groom, arrives with the elders of the family. The bride, her mother, the women, and the girls of Obierika's family shake hands with the guests. Then Obierika presents kola nuts as a symbol of hospitality to his in-laws. His eldest brother breaks the first kola nut and says, ". . . let there be friendship between your family and ours." (p. 82) The in-laws respond, "You are a great family of prosperous men and great warriors." (p. 82) The two families celebrate with a great feast. The young men sing praise songs, and Okonkwo is lauded as the greatest wrestler and warrior alive. The young girls and the bride dance. Finally, Ibe takes his bride home to spend seven market weeks with his family. The in-laws sing songs and pay their respects to prominent men like Okonkwo as they leave.

Analysis

In the beginning of the chapter, Okonkwo is depicted as a humble father powerless in the face of his god. He submits to Agbala's will, and he patiently travels to the hills and caves four times in order to assist his wife Ekwefi and his daughter Ezinma. This portrait is contrasted with Okonkwo at the end of the chapter where he is praised as a great wrestler, warrior, and prominent leader. The betrothal of Obierika's daughter illustrates the author's view of a woman's role in Igbo society. A woman who increases her husband's lineage is respected because children are considered a reincarnation of the ancestors and protection against poverty in old age. The *uri* is a woman's ceremony and contrasts with the trial of Uzowulu, which is a man's ceremony. However, Achebe has been criticized for his treatment of women in the novel. Some critics feel his female characters are portrayed like possessions who are bought and sold by polygamous men. The incident concerning the cow may be an attempt to portray the *otu omu*, a women's council that controls the local marketplace by imposing fines on anyone who disturbs the peace. However, in his re-creation of Igbo life, Achebe does not emphasize the political role of women. In the traditional Igbo world, women not only regulated markets, but also settled civil and marital disputes.

Study Questions

1. How do the people of Umuike develop their market?
2. The story of the man and the goat shows that the Umuike market is often filled with thieves. What happens in this story?

3. What do Okonkwo's first and third wives contribute to the betrothal feast?

4. Why does Ekwefi join the betrothal feast later?

5. The members of Obierika's extended family sit in a half-moon. When his in-laws arrive, they complete the circle. What is the significance of the seating arrangement?

6. Describe the difference in the attire of the married women and that of the girls who greet the in-laws.

7. What does the eldest man among the in-laws mean when he says, "This is not the first time my people have come to marry your daughter"? (p. 83)

8. Why does Obierika's family say their daughter will be a good wife and bear nine sons?

9. What kinds of men are respected and praised by Obierika's in-laws?

10. How do you know that Okonkwo is a respected member of Obierika's extended family?

Answers

1. The people of Umuike make a powerful medicine. It takes the form of an old woman who beckons the neighboring clans to the market.

2. Once a man went to lead a goat by a thick rope to the Umuike market. Someone stole the goat and replaced it with a heavy log of wood.

3. Nwoye's mother and Ojiugo, Okonkwo's youngest wife, take cocoyams, salt, smoked fish, plantains, palm oil, and water to the betrothal feast.

4. Ekwefi is exhausted from the previous night.

5. The two families unite as one as they sit in a complete circle together.

6. The married women wear their best clothes, and the girls wear red and black waist beads and anklets of brass.

7. The eldest man among the in-laws means that his mother came from Obierika's family.

8. Obierika's family says that their daughter will be a good wife and bear nine sons because the role of wife and mother is extremely important for women in Igbo society. The nine sons represent the nine villages of Umuofia and the nine founding fathers of the clan.

9. The in-laws respect and praise men who are great farmers, orators, wrestlers, and warriors.

10. We know that Okonkwo is a respected member of Obierika's extended family because the in-laws look in his direction when they are praising the great men of the family. They also pay him a short courtesy visit before they leave the feast.

Suggested Essay Topics

1. Describe the role of women in Igbo society based on the information you have gathered in this chapter. Discuss the role of women in the family, women in religion, and women in politics.

2. Explain how Achebe complicates the character of Okonkwo. Compare Okonkwo on the dark night he waited for Ezinma at the cave of Agbala with Okonkwo on the day he accompanied his adopted son, Ikemefuna, through the forest.

Chapter Thirteen

Summary

Ezeudu, one of the oldest men in the clan, is dead. The last time Ezeudu visited Okonkwo, he told him not to participate in Ikemefuna's death because the boy called him father. Ezeudu was a great man, and he is given a warrior's funeral. The drums of death are beaten, and the guns are fired. Warriors painted with chalk and charcoal assemble in age groups wearing smoked raffia shirts. Several ancestral spirits or *egwugwu* appear from the underworld speaking in unearthly voices. Some *egwugwu*, like Evil Spirit, are violent and have to be restrained. There is another dreaded *egwugwu* who is always alone. He is shaped like a coffin; a sickly odor hangs in the air, and flies travel with him. Even the greatest medicine men retire when he passes. He has one hand and carries a basket full of water. Other *egwugwu*, however, are harmless. Another one is so old, he leans heavily on a stick. He walks to the corpse, gazes at it awhile, and then disappears into the underworld.

It is a great funeral, and everyone in the clan participates. The men shout, fire guns, beat drums, and clash their machetes. They celebrate the life of Ezeudu, who has taken three titles. This is a rare achievement because there are only four titles in the clan. Only one or two men in any generation ever achieve the fourth and highest title. When they do, they become lords of the land. Before Ezeudu is buried, the tumult increases tenfold. Drums beat violently, and men leap up and down in a frenzy. The drums and dancing reach fever pitch. Then an anguished cry comes from the center of the fury. Everyone is silent like a spell has been cast. Ezeudu's 16-year-old son lies dead in a pool of blood. He has been dancing the traditional farewell to his father with his brothers and half-brothers. Okonkwo is responsible; his gun has exploded accidentally, and a piece of iron has pierced the boy's heart. Nothing like this has ever happened in Umuofia before.

It is a crime against the Earth goddess to kill a clansman. There are two types of crimes, male and female. Okonkwo has committed a female crime because the murder is an accident. Nevertheless, he is forced to flee from the clan. He may return after seven years. Okonkwo collects his belongings, and his wives and children weep bitterly. Obierika stores his yams, and Okonkwo and his family flee to his motherland. It is a little village called Mbanta, just beyond the borders of Mbaino. The next day, a crowd of men from Ezeudu's quarter storm into Okonkwo's compound dressed in war regalia. The men set fire to his houses, demolish his walls, kill his animals, and destroy his barn. There is no malice in their hearts; they are simply messengers administering the justice of Ani, the Earth goddess. They are cleansing the land that Okonkwo has polluted with the blood of a clansman.

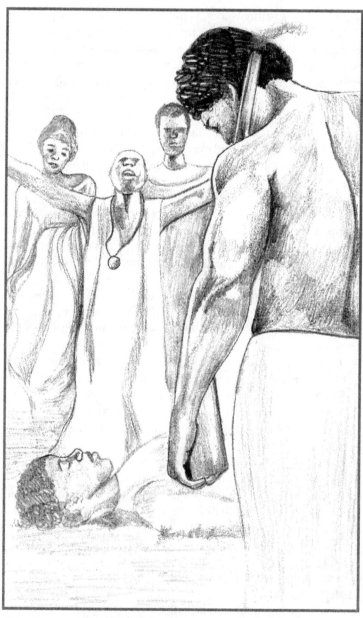

Okonkwo accidentally kills Ezeudu's son at the funeral.

Obierika, Okonkwo's greatest friend, is among the men who raze his compound. Obierika is a man who thinks about things. He mourns his friend's calamity and wonders why a man should suffer so grievously for an offense he has committed inadvertently. He remembers his wife's twins, whom he had thrown away, and he wonders what crime the infants committed. Yet, the earth goddess decreed that twins were an offense of the land and must be destroyed. If the clan did not exact punishment for an offense against the great goddess, her wrath would be unleashed upon everyone, not just the offender.

Analysis

Ezeudu is an example of a great Igbo who has taken three titles. The Igbo system allows talented men to proclaim their prestige and power by purchasing titles. The process requires a general consensus of the community, and the titles allow men greater participation in political and religious life. Great men who achieve the highest title undergo a ritual death and resurrection during their lifetime. As the great elder Ezeudu physically passes over the threshold of death into the afterlife, the community is reminded that the spirit world is not far removed from the land of the living. The *egwugwu* illustrate the domain of the ancestors, for the spirits of the dead travel freely between the two worlds, especially at festivals and funerals.

It is ironic that Ezeudu, the elder who told Okonkwo to refrain from killing Ikemefuna, now loses a son to Okonkwo. Defending himself from appearing weak, Okonkwo deliberately killed Ikemefuna. At Ezeudu's funeral, however, Okonkwo accidentally kills Ezeudu's 16-year-old son. This is considered involuntary manslaughter, which is a female crime. The male crime would have been premeditated murder. Nevertheless, the killing of Ezeudu's son is the last in a long list of offenses Okonkwo has committed against the Earth goddess and the traditional moral order of the Igbo people. Okonkwo beat his youngest wife, Ojiugo, during the Week of Peace; he took a shot at his second wife, Ekwefi, before the Yam Festival; and he participated in the ritual murder of his adopted son, Ikemefuna. Okonkwo also beat his son Nwoye and disdained unsuccessful men in the community. Okonkwo has committed many offenses; now he is banished to his mother's homeland because he accidentally killed a clansman. It is ironic that Okonkwo, a man who committed many acts of violence, is punished for an accident.

Obierika helps Okonkwo by storing his yams; he also participates in razing Okonkwo's compound to the ground. Again, Obierika illustrates the complexity of the Igbo moral code. Obierika is described as a man who thinks about things. In some ways, he presents a foil to Okonkwo, who is an unreflective man of action. Although Obierika feels that Okonkwo's banishment is extremely harsh punishment, he accepts Ani's mandate. However, Obierika questions the traditional order as he did after Ikemefuna's death. He mourns Okonkwo's banishment and remembers the twins he abandoned in the forest. Some critics believe Achebe uses Obierika as the center of consciousness at this point.

As Part One of the novel ends, Okonkwo has failed because he has not been faithful to the moral code of traditional Igbo life. His crimes stem from a lack of balance between masculine and feminine energies; as a result he cannot balance his personal achievements and quest for success with his responsibilities to the community at large. Okonkwo may be a victim of his ill-fated *chi*. His downfall may also represent the disintegration of traditional Igbo life and serve as a foreshadowing of the profound change Igbo society will undergo at the hands of the British colonial powers.

Study Questions

1. What is the role of the esoteric language of the *ekwe*, or the drum?

2. What is the name of the clan, and what villages are part of the clan?

3. What is the name of Okonkwo's village?

4. How do the men express their anguish at Ezeudu's death?

5. What does the one-handed spirit mean when he asks Ezeudu to come again the way he came before?

6. How does Okonkwo accidentally kill Ezeudu's son during the farewell dance?

7. Why do Okonkwo and his family leave their homestead?

8. Where do Okonkwo and his family go?

9. Why does Obierika begin to wonder about the justice of the Earth goddess?

10. What do the elders mean when they say "If one finger brought oil it soiled the others"? (p. 88)

Answers

1. The esoteric language of the *ekwe,* or the drum, carries the news of Ezeudu's death to all nine villages of Umuofia and beyond.

2. The name of the clan is Umuofia. The clan includes all the members of the nine villages of Umuofia.

3. Okonkwo's village is Iguedo.

4. The men dash around in a frenzy, cutting down trees and animals, jumping over walls, and dancing on the roof.

5. Ezeudu is lacking nothing. He is rich, brave, and he lived a long life. The one-handed spirit asks Ezeudu to come back to Earth this way again.

6. Okonkwo accidentally kills Ezeudu's son when his gun goes off by mistake as the men are clashing their machetes.

7. Okonkwo and his family are banished from the village for seven years because Okonkwo accidentally kills a clansman.

8. Okonkwo and his family flee to Okonkwo's mother's village.

9. Obierika wonders about the justice of the Earth goddess because Okonkwo is banished for seven years for a crime he committed by mistake. Obierika also wonders about the justice of abandoning twins in the forest.

10. The elders mean if one person in the clan commits a crime, they bring the wrath of the Earth goddess upon all the members of the clan.

Suggested Essay Topics

1. Explain why Ezeudu is such an important and well-respected man in Umuofia. Discuss his family, his finances, his political power, and his role in the community. Explain how Ezeudu interpreted the decrees of the Earth goddess in terms of Okonkwo's responsibility to his adopted son, Ikemefuna.

2. Obierika is a thoughtful, well-balanced Igbo. Explain how Obierika can question the justice of the Earth goddess, support Okonkwo by storing his yams, and raze his friend's homestead at the same time.

Part Two

Chapter Fourteen

New Characters:

Uchendu: *Okonkwo's uncle; his mother's brother*

Amikwu: *the youngest of Uchendu's five sons*

Njide: *Uchendu's eldest daughter*

Akeuni: *Uchendu's daughter who has borne and thrown away many twins*

Summary

Part Two takes place in Mbanta, the home of Okonkwo's mother. Okonkwo's crime of killing Ezeudu's son is involuntary manslaughter, a female *ochu*. Okonkwo is banished by Ani, the Earth goddess, to Mbanta for seven years. Uchendu, Okonkwo's mother's brother, arranges the rites of purification. Okonkwo is given land for his homestead and farm. He works hard, but work no longer holds any pleasure for him. The passion to become one of the lords of the clan has ruled his life. He almost achieved it, and then everything was shattered. His personal god, or *chi*, is not made for great things. Okonkwo is bowed with grief and sorrow.

The entire extended family, or the *umunna*, meets to celebrate the *isa-ifi* ceremony for Amikwu, Uchendu's youngest son. Amikwu is marrying a new wife, and this ceremony determines the faithfulness of a woman who has been separated from her fiancé for a long period of time. Njide, Uchendu's eldest daughter, asks the bride how many men she has lain with since Amikwu expressed his desire to marry her. She said she has not lain with any other men. Amikwu takes the young bride to his home, and she becomes his wife.

Uchendu takes the opportunity to speak. He confirms that Okonkwo is an exile condemned to live in a strange land for seven years. He also confirms that a man and his children belong in their fatherland. Yet, he reminds Okonkwo that his mother is buried in Mbanta. Uchendu asks Okonkwo why the Igbo people give their children the name "Nneka" or "Mother is Supreme." Okonkwo does not know the answer. Uchendu then asks Okonkwo why a woman is buried in her parent's home with her own kinsmen. Again, Okonkwo does not know the answer. Uchendu tells Okonkwo that he is like a child. He explains that when a father beats a child, it seeks sympathy in its mother's hut. He said that a man belongs to his fatherland when life is good, but when there is sorrow and bitterness, a man finds refuge in his motherland. Mother is there to protect the child. That is why the Igbo say, "Mother is Supreme." (p. 94)

Uchendu tells Okonkwo he is not the greatest sufferer in the world. He explains that some men lose all their yams, and some are banished for life. Uchendu had six wives; they are all dead now except one. He has buried 22 children, yet he has not hung himself. His daughter Akeuni has also suffered because she has abandoned many twins. Uchendu explains that Okonkwo's duty is to comfort his wives and children; otherwise, his family will die in exile. Okonkwo must accept his cousins as his kinsmen. Uchendu concludes his message to Okonkwo, saying, "I have no more to say to you." (p. 95)

Analysis

This chapter illustrates the maternal lines of land entitlement among the Igbo, for Okonkwo is entitled to land in his mother's village. The backdrop for the chapter is the betrothal and marriage customs of the Igbo people. This is the third marriage described in the novel. The ceremony focuses on proving the fidelity of the new

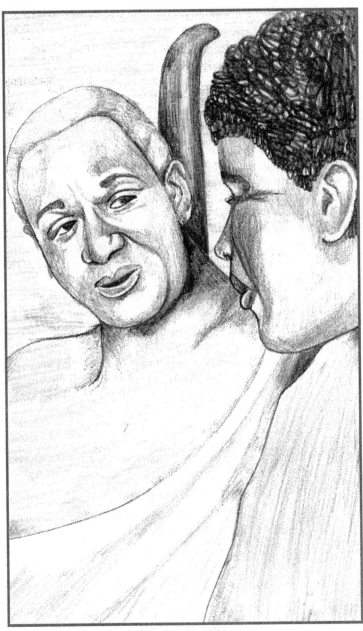

The elder Uchendu welcomes his nephew Okonkwo in Mbanta and explains that a Mother's love is supreme.

wife; there is no such ritual to ascertain the groom's fidelity. The marriage provides an opportunity for Uchendu to speak. Uchendu's dialogue with Okonkwo illustrates Okonkwo's inability to grasp the concept of the feminine principle in the Igbo world view. Okonkwo basically rejects the feminine principle represented by Mbanta and refuses the comfort of his motherland. He also rejects the civil culture the feminine principle regulates.

Okonkwo's main objective in life is to become a respected leader in the clan. Work is his passion and life-spring, and now work holds no meaning for him. Okonkwo seeks to amass wealth, demonstrate personal achievement, and acquire prestigious titles. He has earned two titles and was chosen as an *egwugwu* representing clan's ancestors. Okonkwo is bitter about his exile in Mbanta because he is delayed in achieving his goals. Although Okonkwo works hard, he realizes that a man cannot rise above the destiny of his *chi*. Therefore, he wallows in depression and self-pity and is rebuked by Uchendu.

While Okonkwo experiences the bitterness of exile, he has the opportunity to take refuge with the feminine principle and learn the supremacy of a mother's nurturing love. Uchendu tells Okonkwo and the entire extended family that "Mother is Supreme." (p. 94) This truth sets the tone for Part Two of the novel. However, Okonkwo never internalizes this truth.

Study Questions

1. Why does Okonkwo seek refuge in his motherland?

2. What is the frozen water called "the nuts of the water of heaven"? (p. 92)

3. How does Okonkwo start his yam farm in Mbanta?

4. How does Okonkwo feel about the elders' belief that if a man says "yes," his *chi* will also affirm him?

5. Explain the significance of the *isa-ifi* ceremony.

6. How does Uchendu establish his authority when he addresses Okonkwo?

7. Why was the name "Nneka," or "Mother is Supreme," a common name among the Igbo people?

8. According to Uchendu, what is Okonkwo's duty and responsibility during his time of exile?

9. What is the meaning of the song the Igbo people sing when a woman dies that says, "For whom is it well, for whom is it well? There is no one for whom it is well." (p. 95)

10. Why does Uchendu have nothing else to say to Okonkwo?

Answers

1. Okonkwo seeks refuge in his motherland because he accidentally killed a clansman; he is banished by Ani, the Earth goddess.

2. The rain called "the nuts of the water of heaven" is hail. (p. 92)

3. Uchendu has five sons. Each son contributes 300 seed-yams to enable their cousin Okonkwo to plant a farm.

4. Okonkwo feels that the elders' belief is false; he is a man whose *chi* says "no" to greatness despite his own efforts to succeed.

5. The *isa-ifi* ceremony is the final segment in an elaborate wedding rite and establishes the fidelity of the bride. The bride-price has been paid, and all the daughters of the family are present.

6. Uchendu says he is an old man and he knows the world better than the younger people. He asks anyone who knows more about the world to speak up.

7. The name "Nneka," or "Mother is Supreme," is a common name among the Igbo people because a mother's nurturing love is respected. (p. 94)

8. According to Uchendu, Okonkwo's duty is to comfort his wives and children and return them to his fatherland after seven years. Uchendu says if Okonkwo allows sorrow to weigh him down and kill him, his family will die in exile. Okonkwo must accept his cousins as his kinsmen.

9. The song implies that it is not easy for anyone in life. It is difficult for anyone to lose his or her mother.

10. Uchendu implies there is no reason to discuss matters further; Okonkwo needs to reflect on what Uchendu has said.

Suggested Essay Topics

1. Uchendu attempts to convince Okonkwo that he is not the greatest sufferer in the world. Provide three examples Uchendu uses to make his point.

2. Give a detailed analysis of the saying "Mother is Supreme," as it relates to Okonkwo. (p. 94) Use three examples to support your points.

Chapter Fifteen

New Character:

Nweke: *a young man who accompanies Obierika*

Summary

Two years after Okonkwo's banishment to Mbanta, his friend Obierika comes to visit him. He is accompanied by two young men carrying heavy bags of cowries. Obierika tells Okonkwo that the clan of Abame has been wiped out. Fugitives from Abame explained that a white man appeared. The Oracle explained that the strange man would break their clan and spread destruction among them. The Igbos of Abame killed the white man and tied his iron horse to a sacred tree. He said a word that resembled *Mbaino*. Perhaps he had been traveling to Mbaino and lost his way. Sometime later, three white men led by a band of ordinary men like the Igbo of Umofia came to the clan. They saw the iron horse and went away. Nothing happened for many weeks. Then on the market day when the whole clan was gathered together, the men surrounded the market. They shot and killed just about everyone in the clan.

Uchendu says the men of Abame were fools because they should not have killed a man who said nothing. He tells a story about a mother bird and her daughter to illustrate his point. Okonkwo agrees that the men should have been more vigilant; they had been warned of danger. Obierika expresses fear because the Igbo have heard stories about armed white men who sell Igbos into slavery.

Nwoye's mother cooks a fine meal; Ezinma brings a bowl of water for the guests to wash their hands, and Nwoye serves wine. Obierika finally explains that the heavy bags contain money from Okonkwo's yams. Obierika sold the large yams and some of the seed-yams; he gave other yams to sharecroppers. Obierika promises to sell the yams every year until Okonkwo returns. Okonkwo is overwhelmed by his friend's goodness and cannot thank him enough. Obierika jokes and says, "Kill one of your sons for me." (p. 100) When Okonkwo replies that would be inadequate, Obierika responds, "Then kill yourself." (p. 100) Okonkwo asks his friend to forgive him.

Analysis

The changes that occur while Okonkwo is in exile in Mbanta reflect the dawn of the colonial period in Nigeria. In the nineteenth century, the Igbo traded palm oil for European goods. However, friendly relations with the British eventually crumbled, and pockets of violence erupted along the Niger River. In order to "pacify" Eastern Nigeria, the British destroyed much of Igboland and launched extensive military expeditions. Although the Igbo people resisted, the twentieth century saw the dawn of British imperialism. The fictional incident of the white man with an iron horse is directly drawn from the murder of J. F. Stewart on November 26, 1905. This historical event led to the destruction of the village of Ahiara, which in turn led to the pacification of the Igbo people in areas around Onitsha. The destruction of Abame reflects this historical event in the novel.

This chapter also illustrates Obierika's loyal friendship. Not only does Obierika act as a steward of Okonkwo's fortune in yams, he also acts as a link between Okonkwo's clan and Mbanta. It is Obierika who keeps Okonkwo abreast of the events in Umuofia during his exile. Obierika provides invaluable information for Okonkwo and the reader. The joking between the friends at the end of the chapter provides foreshadowing of the denouement of the novel. It is interesting that Okonkwo does not view Obierika's empathy and kindness as feminine weakness in this case.

Study Questions

1. Why does Uchendu say that Obierika's generation stays at home and even a man's motherland is strange to him?

2. What are the names of some of the clans Uchendu knows in the area?

3. What did the fearless men of Abame do when they met the white man?

4. Why did the Oracle say the white men were like locusts?

5. Why did the white man seem to speak through his nose?

6. Why did the white men wait for the market day to slaughter Abame?

7. Give an example proving that a great evil descended upon Abame just as the Oracle warned.

8. What is the significance of the story of Mother Kite, the bird?

9. Why does Obierika get a late start on his journey?

10. Why does Obierika bring Okonkwo the money?

Answers

1. The younger generation does not travel to distant clans. They are so afraid of their neighbors, they do not even visit their mothers' homes.

2. Some of the clans Uchendu knows in the area are Aninta, Umuazu, Ikeocha, Elumelu, and Abame.

3. The fearless men of Abame touched and killed the white man.

4. The Oracle said the white men were like locusts because the first one was a scout who was sent to explore the terrain. Other white men would follow him.

5. The white man seemed to speak through his nose because his language and intonation were unfamiliar to the Igbo people.

6. The white men waited for the big market day to slaughter the people of Abame because almost every person in the clan was in the market.

7. The sacred fish in the mysterious lake of Abame fled, and the lake turned the color of blood.

8. Mother Kite sent her daughter for food. The mother duck did not cry when she seized her duckling, but the mother chicken did cry when she seized her chick. Mother Kite sent the duckling back but kept the chick.

9. Obierika means to set out before the cock crowed, but Nweke, one of the men accompanying him, is late. Obierika says you should never make an early morning appointment with a man who has just married a new wife.

10. Obierika brings Okonkwo the money because he thinks Okonkwo might need it. Obierika does not know what might happen tomorrow. The clan may be invaded by green men who will shoot them.

Suggested Essay Topics

1. Give a detailed example explaining how Obierika is a good and loyal friend to Okonkwo.

2. Why does Uchendu tell the story of Mother Kite? Give three reasons to support your points.

Chapter Sixteen

Summary

Two years later, Obierika visits Okonkwo again. He has seen Nwoye among the missionaries in Umuofia. They have built a church and won a handful of converts. The converts are

The first Igbo Christians are *osu*, outcasts, mothers of twins, and
weak, unsuccessful men who are considered worthless by the clan.

considered to be *efulefu*, or worthless men, by the Igbo community. The missionaries have also come to Mbanta. One is a white
man who speaks through an interpreter. He preaches about a new
God, the Creator of all the world. He says this God judges the dead.
Good men who worship the true God live forever. Evil men who
worship wood and stone are thrown into an eternal fire.

An old man asks if the Christian God is the goddess of the Earth,
the god of the sky, or Amadiora. He asks about protection from the
anger of the neglected gods and ancestors. The missionary says
the Igbo deities are deceitful and teach the people to kill one another and destroy innocent children. He preaches about one true
God who created the earth, the sky, and all humankind. The Igbo
gods are simply wood and stone. The men of Mbanta break into
derisive laughter. They think the missionary is mad; otherwise, he
would never say that Ani, Idemili, Ogwugwu, and Amadiora are
harmless.

Then the missionary bursts into song. The interpreter explains
each verse. He sings about a brother who lives in darkness, fear,
and the ignorance of God's love. He sings about a sheep on the hills
away from the tender shepherd's care. Then, the interpreter speaks
about the Son of God named Jesu Kristi. A man challenges him—
first he preaches about one God; then he teaches about his son.
One Igbo reasons that God must have a wife, and the crowd agrees.
The interpreter's response is confused. He is from a different region and speaks a different dialect. Instead of referring to himself
as "myself," he refers to himself as "my buttocks." (p. 102) This
makes everyone laugh. When the missionary continues preaching
about the Holy Trinity, Okonkwo thinks he is mad.

However, Nwoye has been captivated by the poetry of the new
religion. It touches something in the marrow of his bones. The
hymn about brothers who sit in darkness and fear seems to answer a vague and persistent question that has haunted his soul. It
is the question of the twins crying in the bush and the question of
Ikemefuna, who was killed. When Obierika sees Nwoye among the
Christians in Umuofia, Nwoye tells him he no longer knows his
father, Okonkwo.

Analysis

The arrival of the Europeans alters the fabric of economic, political, and social life; Christian missionaries simultaneously offer respite to the disenfranchised among the Igbo and attack the foundation of traditional Igbo religion. The Anglican Church Missionary Society established a mission in Onitsha in 1857; later the Roman Catholic Holy Ghost Fathers and the Society of African Missions set up stations east and west of the Niger River. Christianity offered a message of love to those who did not succeed in the Igbo world. The first converts included those who felt disenfranchised: the anguished mothers of twins, who had been forced to abandon their children; the *osu*, who were despised as descendants of religious slave cults; and the men who did not earn titles and achieve traditional wealth and status.

Although Christianity offered respite to the marginalized, the new faith tore apart the fabric of traditional Igbo life. The missionaries preached the mystery of the Trinity but could not understand the Igbo concept of a multidimensional God. The Christians reenacted the Last Supper but could not accept the rituals performed by the *egwugwu*, or masked elders, who ritually represented the ancestral spirits of the village. In addition to the religious dogma, the missionaries condemned polygamy and other traditional Igbo customs.

Study Questions

1. How do the leaders of Umuofia feel about the new religion?

2. What does Chielo, the priestess of Agbala, mean when she calls the converts "the excrement of the clan"? (p. 101)

3. Why doesn't Okonkwo want to speak to Obierika about Nwoye?

4. Why do the Igbo people laugh at the interpreter even though he is speaking Igbo?

5. What is an iron horse?

6. Why are the people excited by what the missionary says?

7. Why do the men of Umuofia laugh at the missionary?

8. Why does Okonkwo stay and listen to the missionary?

9. How does the interpreter explain that the true God has a son but no wife?

10. How does Nwoye feel when he hears the Christians' hymn?

Answers

1. Christianity is a source of great sorrow to the leaders of Umuofia, but many believe the faith will not last.

2. When Chielo calls the converts "the excrement of the clan," she means that they are the outcasts and the lowest members of the clan. (p. 101)

3. Okonkwo does not want to speak to Obierika about Nwoye because he is so furious with his son. Obierika learns the story from Nwoye's mother.

4. The interpreter is from a different region, and he speaks a different dialect. Instead of referring to himself as "myself," he refers to himself as "my buttocks." This makes everyone laugh. (p. 102)

5. An iron horse is a bicycle.

6. The people are excited because the missionary says he is going to live with the Igbo people.

7. The men of Umuofia laugh at the missionary when he says that all the Igbo gods are harmless.

8. Okonkwo stays and listens to the missionary because he hopes the Igbo people will chase him out of town or whip him.

9. The interpreter cannot explain why the Christian God has a son but no wife.

10. When he hears the Christians' hymn, Nwoye feels relief pouring into his parched soul. The words of the hymn are like the drops of frozen rain melting on the dry earth.

Suggested Essay Topics

1. An *efulefu* is a man who sells his machete and wears only his sheath into battle. Is the *efulefu* a good representation of the Igbo men and women who were first attracted to Christianity? Provide at least three examples to support your point.

2. Explain how Christianity exacerbates the relationship between Nwoye and Okonkwo.

Chapter Seventeen

New Characters:

Mr. Kiaga: *Igbo interpreter for the missionaries*

Nneka: *the wife of the prosperous farmer Amadi*

Summary

When the Christians ask the Igbo for a plot of land to build a church, the elders offer them the Evil Forest, which is filled with sinister forces. The Igbos know the gods and ancestors of Mbanta have a limit; they expected the missionaries to be punished by the seventh market week. However, the missionaries live on, and they build a new house for their teacher, Mr. Kiaga.

Nwoye is secretly interested in the new faith, and he listens when the missionaries preach in the open marketplace. He learns some of the simple stories. Mr. Kiaga tells the people to come every seventh day to worship the true God. Nwoye hears their loud and confident singing. One of the new converts is Nneka, who is heavy with child. She is the wife of Amadi, a prosperous farmer. Nneka has had four previous pregnancies. Each time she bore twins, and the infants had been thrown away. Her husband and family consider her rubbish.

Okonkwo hears about Nwoye's interest in Christianity and beats him savagely. Uchendu orders him to release the boy, and Nwoye leaves his homestead forever. He tells Mr. Kiaga that he has decided to go to Umuofia, where the missionaries have set up a Christian school. Okonkwo wants to take his machete and wipe out the vile Christians, but he tells himself that Nwoye is not worth the fight. He wonders about the curse of his son. He blames the great misfortune of his exile and now his despicable son's behavior upon his *chi*. Nwoye's crime is an abomination. He has abandoned the gods of his ancestors. Okonkwo is deeply worried that all his male children will follow Nwoye's steps. A cold shudder runs through him at the terrible prospect. It is the prospect of annihilation. He sees himself and his father crowded around their ancestral shrine; they are waiting in vain for worship and sacrifice and find nothing but the ashes of bygone days. He envisions his children praying to the white man's God. If such a thing happens, he will wipe his descendants off the face of the earth. Okonkwo wonders how he could have begotten a son like Nwoye who is such a degenerate and so clearly resembles his father, Unoka.

Analysis

Okonkwo has hoped to achieve immortality by taking the highest title in the land. The *ozo* title achieves ritual death and resurrection for an individual during his lifetime. Okonkwo has not been able to achieve this title. Therefore, as a departed ancestor, he will expect his sons to pour libations or offerings to him before drinking palm wine. He will expect a piece of kola nut to be offered in his name as his sons ask for his protection and guidance. Okonkwo also will expect his descendants to offer animal sacrifices in his name. In this way, Okonkwo will achieve immortality, and his memory will live on.

If Nwoye and the rest of his children turn away from the traditional Igbo religion, Okonkwo will never achieve immortality and live on in the memory of his children. His children will never offer him traditional sacrifices. Okonkwo sees things falling apart. The new religion is destroying the fabric of Igbo life. Okonkwo is angry and afraid because his belief system, his values, and his entire way of life are being challenged by the white man and the new religion. If this religion takes hold, the Igbo will not live on after death.

Study Questions

1. What difficulty do the missionaries encounter when they try to speak to the leaders of the village?

2. Describe the Evil Forest.

3. Why is the Evil Forest a strange site for the missionary's church?

4. Why does Nneka convert to Christianity?

5. Why do some converts suspend their new faith until after the seventh market week?

6. Where does the white missionary go when he leaves Mbanta?

7. Why does it seem like the Evil Forest is going to gobble up the church?

8. What does Mr. Kiaga refer to when he says, "Blessed is he who forsakes his father and his mother for my sake....Those that hear my words are my father and my mother"? (p. 108)

9. According to Okonkwo, what is Nwoye's crime?

10. Why is Okonkwo called "Roaring Flame"?

Answers

1. The missionaries ask for the king of the village, but there is no king. Mbanta is ruled by men of high title, the chief priests, and the elders.

2. Every clan and village has an Evil Forest where they bury those who die of diseases like leprosy and smallpox. The Evil Forest is a dumping ground for the potent fetishes of great medicine men when they die.

3. It is a strange site for the church because it is an evil place, filled with sinister forces.

4. Nneka converts to Christianity because she gave birth to four sets of twins, and all the children have been abandoned in the Evil Forest. She is pregnant again.

5. Some of the converts suspend their new faith until after the seventh market week because they are afraid the gods and ancestors will wipe out the missionaries.

6. The white missionary goes back to build his headquarters in Umuofia. He pays regular visits to the congregation at Mbanta.

7. The church stands on a circular clearing. It looks like the open mouth of the Evil Forest is waiting to snap its teeth together and destroy the church.

8. Mr. Kiaga is referring to a passage in the New Testament. Nwoye does not really understand what Mr. Kiaga is saying, but he is happy to leave his father.

9. Okonkwo feels that Nwoye is abandoning the gods of his ancestors and acting like an effeminate old man.

10. Okonkwo is called "Roaring Flame" because he is fiery and powerful. He concludes that "Living fire begets cold, impotent ash." (p. 109) As he is living fire, Nwoye is cold ash.

Suggested Essay Topics

1. Explain why Nwoye's interest in Christianity may result in the annihilation of Okonkwo and his ancestors. Provide two quotes to support your points.

2. As he stares into the fire, Okonkwo ponders Nwoye's behavior. He wonders how a man like himself could father a weak and useless son like Nwoye. What is Okonkwo's analysis of the situation?

Chapter Eighteen

New Characters:

Okeke: *a man in Mbanta; interpreter for Mr. Smith*

Mr. Brown: *the white missionary*

Okoli: *a convert who kills the sacred python*

Summary

The clan is not too worried about the church. The Christians rescue twins from the bush but never bring them to the village. Some converts are beaten after boasting that the Igbo gods are dead. Otherwise, there is little interaction between the church and the clan. Mr. Kiaga is quite harmless, and anyone who kills a convert will be forced into exile. If the Christians become more troublesome, they will simply be driven out of the clan.

The little church is absorbed in its own troubles. The Christians protest admitting the *osu* or the outcasts of society. Mr. Kiaga explains that there is no slave before God, and the *osu* need Christ. He is a source of inspiration and confidence for the young church. Therefore, several *osu* shave off their long, dirty hair, and some become strong adherents of the new faith. Most of the *osu* in Mbanta join the church. One *osu* named Okoli has so much zeal, he kills a sacred python. No one actually sees him do it, but the leaders of Mbanta are furious. Okonkwo wants to expel the Christians from the village. Others are afraid to get involved. Okonkwo feels the Christians are pouring filth over them daily. He thinks Mbanta is a womanly clan. Such a thing would never happen in Umuofia. The villagers decide to ostracize the Christians so they will not be held accountable for their abominations.

Nevertheless, the Christians are confident. Mr. Brown, the white missionary, pays regular visits to the community. During holy week, the women scrub the church. Some go to the stream to get water; some go to the red-earth pit to get earth; and others go to the quarry to get chalk. However, all of the women are chased back; some of them are whipped. Mr. Kiaga is perplexed. The villagers explain that the Christians have been outlawed because Okoli killed the sacred python. Okoli denies it. He soon falls ill; by the end of the day, Okoli is dead. This proves that the Igbo gods are alive.

Analysis

Each *diala*, or freeborn individual, has the right to climb to the top of Igbo society. The only barrier to achieving success is the payment of membership fees in order to secure titles and enter various societies. However, the *osu* is a contradiction of the Igbo egalitarian ideology. The *osu* is a slave cult dedicated to a deity, and an individual *osu* is a slave dedicated to a god. An *osu* cannot marry or be married by a free Igbo. He lives close to his shrine, and he carries the mark of his forbidden caste—long, tangled, and dirty hair. An *osu* cannot attend meetings, and he cannot take any of the four titles in the clan. When he dies, he is buried in the Evil

The Christians are outlawed because one of the converts kills a sacred python.

Forest. The slave plays an indispensable ritual role and poses a dilemma for the freeborn. The *osu* serve a deity and carry the sins of a freeborn individual. Therefore, the *osu* functions as a special priest, but he is not accorded high status. Furthermore, the freeborn do not know how to interact with the *osu* without offending the deity he serves. As a result, all *osu* are hated, despised, and feared because they remind the freeborn of their guilt. As outcasts, they are treated with horror and contempt. Generally, there is no relationship between the freeborn and the *osu*. These outcasts are among the first Igbos to accept Christianity, Western education, and economic opportunities offered by the colonial powers. As a result, the *osu* are among the best-educated Igbos in the colonial world.

This chapter illustrates the tension created by the *osu* in the infant Christian congregation in Mbanta. The zeal with which the *osu* receive the new religion exacerbates the relationship between the Igbo Christians and the traditional Igbo community. The situation of the *osu* is related to other internal issues that may have contributed to the breakdown of traditional Igbo life. Achebe does not romanticize the past. In fact, some critics feel he is pointing out weaknesses in traditional Igbo society; others feel Achebe reveals his own Christian bias as a Westernized male writing in 1958. For example, Achebe may identify the treatment of the *osu*, the abandonment of twins, ritual sacrifice, and disdain for unsuccessful men as weaknesses within traditional Igbo society. On the other hand, he may identify these elements as aspects of Igbo society that provoke the Europeans to "pacify" and "civilize" the Igbo "savages." The Igbo people are flexible and capable of change. For example, the people phase out the custom of collecting heads in battle, yet Igbo society does not fall apart because this custom is discontinued. Students must reflect on one of the fundamental questions of the novel: Does the Igbo culture fall apart solely because of external pressures of European Imperialism and Christianity, or are there internal tensions that cause the culture to disintegrate as well?

Study Questions

1. Why do the villagers think the Evil Forest is a good home for the Christians?

2. Why would an Igbo who killed a Christian have to flee from the clan?

3. Why are the Igbo Christians upset about admitting the *osu*?

4. How does Mr. Kiaga react to the *osu*?

5. Why are some of the *osu* afraid to shave off their long hair?

6. How does Mr. Kiaga reason with the *osu* about shaving their dirty hair?

7. Why is the python revered?

8. Why do some villagers want to remain uninvolved in the conflict surrounding Okoli?

9. Okonkwo asks the clan to reason like men. What does he say he would do if a man came into his hut and defecated on the floor?

10. When does Okonkwo grind his teeth and why?

Answers

1. The villagers feel that if a gang of *efulefu* decide to live in the Evil Forest, it is their own affair. The Evil Forest is filled with sinister forces; therefore, it is a good home for such marginal people.

2. Anyone who kills a Christian will be banished because even though Christians are considered worthless, they still belong to the clan.

3. The church is upset about admitting the *osu* because they are outcasts and slaves.

4. Mr. Kiaga says that all people are children of God; there is no slave before God. The church must receive their *osu* brothers, and the *osu* need Christ. On judgment day, God will laugh at the Igbo who ostracize the *osu*.

5. Some of the *osu* are afraid to shave off their long hair because a razor is taboo to them; they are afraid they will die.

6. Mr. Kiaga says he did not die after he built his church in the Evil Forest. He did not die because he took care of twins. He calls the Igbos who speak falsehoods "heathens." He says the word of God is true.

7. The python is revered because it comes from the god of water. No one has ever deliberately killed a python.

8. Some villagers feel they should put their fingers into their ears when a man blasphemes. It is not their custom to fight for their gods.

9. Okonkwo says if a man came into his hut and defecated on the floor, he would not shut his eyes; he would take a stick and break his head.

10. Okonkwo grinds his teeth in disgust during the meeting of the Mbanta elders because they decide not to take violent action against the Christians.

Suggested Essay Topics

1. Describe the *osu* and explain why the young church is upset about allowing the *osu* to join the congregation.

2. Some members of the traditional Igbo community want to persecute the Christians; others take a more moderate stand. Explain the rationale behind the two different reactions to the Christians.

Chapter Nineteen

New Characters:

Unachukwu: *an old man in Okonkwo's mother's clan*

Emefo: *an old man in Okonkwo's mother's clan*

Summary

Okonkwo's exile drags to an end. Even though he prospered in Mbanta, Okonkwo is still bitter; he would have prospered more in Umuofia. In seven years he would have climbed to great heights. Nevertheless, his mother's kinsmen have been very kind to him. He calls the first child born to him in Mbanta Nneka, or "Mother is Supreme." However, two years later he calls his newborn son Nwofia, which means "Begotten in the Wilderness." During his last year in exile, Okonkwo asks Obierika to build him two houses in Umuofia; he will construct the rest of his compound himself. Okonkwo has to delay his return to Umuofia until the dry season in order to pay the full penalty of seven years in exile.

Okonkwo and his wives prepare a great feast to thank his mother's kinsmen. Ekwefi provides the cassava; Nwoye's mother and Ojiugo provide smoked fish, palm oil, and pepper. Okonkwo takes care of the meat and yams. Ekwefi harvests the cassava with Ezinma and Obiageli. They carry long cane baskets, machetes for cutting the soft cassava stems, and little hoes for digging out the roots. The leaves are wet, and Ezinma complains about the cold. Obiageli calls her sister "Salt" because she acts like she will dissolve. The harvesting is easy, and the women carry the cassava to the stream.

Okonkwo shows his gratitude to his mother's people by slaughtering three goats and several chickens. His wives prepare *foo-foo*, yam pottage, and soup. All the *umunna*, or the extended family, are invited. Uchendu breaks the kola nut and prays for Okonkwo and his family. The feast is like a wedding celebration. Okonkwo explains that he could never repay his family because "a child cannot pay for its mother's milk." (p. 117) As the palm wine is drunk, one of the oldest members of the *umunna* rises to thank Okonkwo for his generosity. The feast is bigger than they expected. He says it is good for the younger generation to see a man like Okonkwo doing things in the grand old way. He also says it is good for kinsmen to come together. He expresses fear for the young people because they no longer know how to speak with one voice. Christianity, an abominable religion, has settled among them. Now a man can curse the gods and the ancestors; now a man can leave his father and brothers like a mad dog who suddenly turns on its master. The

Okonkwo shows his gratitude to his mother's people by preparing
a huge feast before he returns home from exile in Mbanta.

elders are fearful for the young people, and they thank Okonkwo for calling the family together.

Analysis

Okonkwo has prospered in his motherland, but even as he prepares to return home, he regrets every day of his exile. He is bitter because he has not achieved the success he could have achieved in the warlike Umuofia. He still feels like the clan in Mbanta is womanly. Okonkwo has not learned the values of the feminine principle. He has not learned the truth that "Mother is Supreme." Okonkwo is no more balanced after his exile than he was when he was banished from Umuofia by the Earth goddess for his crime of accidentally killing Ezeudu's son at the funeral. Okonkwo has not learned to balance his masculine and feminine energies. This is the balance that will help him achieve success in the traditional Igbo world. Okonkwo is still inflexible. He is still focused on personal achievement. Ironically, if Okonkwo were a European, these qualities would most likely result in success.

Furthermore, Okonkwo has alienated his son Nwoye, and he is enraged by the new religion. Okonkwo has not moved with the new economic forces that the Europeans have introduced, and he is not fully aware of the influence the Europeans wield in Umuofia. Okonkwo remains angry after seven years of exile in his motherland.

Study Questions

1. Why does Okonkwo regret his exile so bitterly even though he prospers in his motherland?

2. What is the significance of the names Okonkwo gives the children who were born during his seven years in exile?

3. Why doesn't Obierika build Okonkwo's *obi* or the walls of his compound in Umuofia?

4. Why can't Okonkwo return to Umuofia before the rains stop?

5. Why does Obiageli call Ezinma "Salt" while they harvest the cassava?

6. Why do the women put the cassava in shallow wells?

7. Why does Uchendu throw one of the kola nuts on the ground?

8. Why do some of the family members whistle when the food is laid out?

9. What does Okonkwo mean when he says that "A child cannot pay for its mother's milk"? (p. 117)

10. Why are the elders fearful for the young people?

Answers

1. Okonkwo regrets his exile even though he prospers in his motherland because he feels he would have prospered even more in Umuofia.

2. He names his daughter Nneka or "Mother is Supreme" and his son Nwofia or "Begotten in the Wilderness." Although Okonkwo shows reverence to his kinsmen by naming a child in honor of mother or the feminine principal, he still feels like his mother's home is a wilderness for him.

3. Obierika doesn't build Okonkwo's *obi* or the walls of his compound because a man either has to build these things for himself or inherit them from his father.

4. Okonkwo has to wait until the rains stop because he has to pay the full penalty of seven years in exile.

5. Ezinma dislikes cold water dripping down her back. Obiageli calls Ezinma "Salt" because she is acting like she might dissolve.

6. The women put the cassava in shallow wells so that it will ferment.

7. Uchendu throws one of the kola nuts on the ground to honor the ancestors.

8. The family is surprised at the huge feast Okonkwo prepares for them.

9. Okonkwo means that he cannot repay his kinsmen for sustaining his life.

10. The elders are fearful for the young people because they do not know the value of kinship or how to speak with one voice. The clan is being divided by Christianity.

Suggested Essay Topics

1. What does the elder mean when he says the young people do not know how to speak with one voice? Explain why the elders are fearful for the younger generation.

2. Has Okonkwo learned the supremacy of a mother's love during his exile in Mbanta? Provide three examples to support your point.

Part Three

Chapter Twenty

New Characters:

Ogbuefi Ugonna: *a man who has taken two titles and joined the Christian church*

Oduche: *a man who dies over a land controversy*

Aneto: *a man who kills Oduche and is hanged by the white authorities*

Summary

Seven years is a long time to be away. Okonkwo has lost his place among the nine masked spirits who administer justice in the clan; he has also lost his chance to lead his people against the new religion. Furthermore, Okonkwo has lost time during which he could have taken the highest titles. He is determined to return to Umuofia with a flourish and regain the seven years he has wasted. Therefore, he decides to build a magnificent compound and initiate his sons into the *ozo* society. Okonkwo believes he will be held in high esteem, and he sees himself taking the highest title in the clan.

However, the white man has instituted many changes in Umuofia during the seven years Okonkwo was in exile. The church has attracted some important men like Ogbuefi Ugonna, who had himself taken two titles before he joined the Christians. He is one of the first men to receive Holy Communion, and the white missionary is very proud of him. The white men have also brought their government. A District Commissioner judges cases in court even though he is completely ignorant of Igbo law and custom. The court messengers are called *kotma*, which means "court man," and they are hated in Umuofia because they are arrogant, high-handed foreigners. The *kotma* are also called "Ashy-Buttocks" because they wear ash-colored shorts. The prison is full of men who have violated the white man's law. Some of the prisoners have abandoned twins and some have molested Christians. The *kotma* beat the prisoners and force them to clear the government compound. Some of the prisoners are men who have earned titles, and they are outraged at this treatment.

Okonkwo wants to drive the white men out of Umuofia; he says the people of Abame were foolish because they did not resist. Obierika says it is too late because many of the clan have become Christians, and they are working in the white man's government. There are only two white men in Umuofia, but many of the Igbo people follow their ways and have been given power. They would marshal support, and Umuofia would be wiped out like Abame.

Okonkwo and Obierika discuss a land dispute in which a man named Aneto has been hanged. The white man's court decided that the land belonged to a family named Nnama, who had given much money to the court messengers and interpreter. The white man does not understand Igbo customs about land, and he does not even speak Igbo. The white men and the Christian Igbos denounce the Igbo customs. Yet, the Igbo cannot fight their own brothers. The white man is very clever because he came quietly and peaceably with his religion. The Igbo were amused at his foolishness and allowed him to stay. But now, the Igbo clan can no longer act as one. Obierika explains that Aneto killed Oduche during that land dispute. Aneto fled to Aninta to escape the wrath of the Earth goddess. The Christians told the white man, and he sent his *kotma* to capture Aneto. Aneto and his family were imprisoned. Oduche died, and Aneto was hanged. The family members were released, but they were so humiliated, they could hardly speak about their suffering. Okonkwo and Obierika sit in silence.

Analysis

During the colonial era, the British sought to govern hundreds
of decentralized Igbo villages clustered in various political constructs through a system of indirect rule. Igbo institutions were
replaced with a "native court." This legal system was not administered by Igbo leaders who had earned titles within the community
but rather by appointed warrant chiefs, who derived their power
from a colonial document called a warrant. The British commis-
sioners regulated local affairs through the warrant chiefs, who punished anyone who resisted colonial rule. As a result, the "native
courts" decided cases that had been judged by village elders in the
past. The land dispute between Aneto and Oduche is an example.
Traditionally, the elders would have banished Aneto to his motherland; however, in this case, he was hanged by the white man's
"native court."

The district officers who controlled the native courts had very
little knowledge of Igbo laws and customs. Most of the officials did
not speak Igbo. As a result, many of their decisions violated Igbo
concepts of justice. The district officers were supported by court
clerks and messengers who also held no traditional status in the
village. In many cases these court personnel were imported from
other areas within Igboland and spoke a somewhat foreign dialect. Corruption was rampant throughout the native court system,
and the Igbo people resisted the destruction of indigenous political life.

Study Questions

1. What is the significance of the saying "The clan was like a
   lizard; if it lost its tail it soon grew another"? (p. 121)

2. How is Okonkwo able to grow yams in Umuofia when he is
   actually located in Mbanta?

3. What is a *kotma*?

4. How does Okonkwo want his sons to be raised?

5. Why does Okonkwo regret that Ezinma is a girl?

6. Why is Ezinma able to convince Obiageli, her half-sister, to
   marry in Umuofia?

7. What is the sacrament of Holy Communion called in Igbo?

8. Describe the city of Umuru and explain its significance.

9. The Igbo prisoners sing a song about the "*kotma* of the ashy buttocks." How do the court messengers react to being called "Ashy-Buttocks"? (pp. 123–124)

10. How does Okonkwo compare the people of Abame with the people of Umuofia?

Answers

1. The saying means that if a man left the clan, someone soon filled his place.

2. Every year Obierika distributes Okonkwo's yams to share-croppers.

3. A *kotma* is a "court man." This is derived from the English term. It is also translated as "court messenger."

4. Okonkwo wants his sons to hold their heads high among the Igbo people. He wants his sons to be raised in traditional Igbo culture.

5. Okonkwo regrets that Ezinma is a girl because she alone understands his every mood, and a bond of sympathy has grown between them. She understands things perfectly. If Ezinma were a boy, Okonkwo could teach her more, and their relationship would survive her marriage.

6. Ezinma wields strong influence over Obiageli. The two young women refuse every offer of marriage in Mbanta.

7. The sacrament of Holy Communion is called "Holy Feast" in Igbo. Ogbuefi Ugonna thinks of the feast in terms of eating and drinking. He puts his drinking-horn into his goatskin bag for the occasion.

8. The city of Umuru is located on the Niger River. White men arrived there many years ago and built their center of religion, trade, and government. The *kotma*, or court messengers, come from Umuru.

9. The court messengers do not like to be called "Ashy-But-tocks." They beat the prisoners, but the song spreads in Umuofia.

10. Okonkwo says the men of Umuofia would be cowards to compare themselves with the men of Abame. The fathers of Abame never dared to stand before the ancestors of Umuofia.

Suggested Essay Topics

1. Identify the role and function of the court messengers and explain the native court system. Use the land dispute between Aneto and Oduche to illustrate how the native court system worked.

2. At the end of this chapter, Obierika explains that the white man ". . . has put a knife on the things that held us together and we have fallen apart." (p. 125) Explain the meaning of Obierika's words and provide three examples to support your point.

Chapter Twenty-One

New Characters:

Enoch: a zealous convert; his father is a priest of the snake cult

Akunna: one of the great men of the village

Summary

Okonkwo hates the white man. However, some Igbos are happy because even though the white man has brought a lunatic religion, he has also brought a trading store. The economy is booming due to the trade in palm oil.

Mr. Brown, the white missionary, is very gentle. He restrains the Christians from provoking the clan and preaches against the kind of excess zeal demonstrated by Enoch, who has killed and

eaten a sacred python. The clan has given Mr. Brown a carved el-
ephant tusk as a sign of respect. Akunna, a great man, sends his
son to Mr. Brown's school. The two men often discuss religion
through an interpreter. Mr. Brown says there is one God who made
Heaven and Earth. Akunna says he is Chukwu, who created the
world and other gods. Mr. Brown says there are no other gods; the
carved *ikenga*, which the Igbos call a god, is a piece of wood.
Akunna explains that the *ikenga* is imbued with a man's spirit; the
tree is made by Chukwu. Mr. Brown says that the spiritual head of
the church is God; the human head of the church is in England.
Akunna explains that Chukwu appoints minor gods because his
work is too great for one person. Mr. Brown explains that Chukwu
is not a person; he says the Igbo worship false gods. Akunna replies that the Igbo worship minor gods who are made by Chukwu.
These gods are messengers; the people turn to Chukwu only when
the lesser gods fail. Mr. Brown says the Igbo are afraid of Chukwu
and explain that God is a loving Father who loves those who do
His will. Akunna says that God's will is too profound to be known.

Mr. Brown knows that a frontal attack on the traditional Igbo
religion will fail. Therefore, he builds a school and a small hospital
in Umuofia. He explains that if Umuofia fails to send children to
school, strangers will rule them. This is already happening in the
native court where the District Commissioner is surrounded by
Igbos who speak English. Most of them come from Umuru on the
banks of the Niger River. After a few months in school, a student
could become a court messenger or clerk; some become teachers.
The mission is prestigious because it is linked with the new government. From the beginning, religion and education go hand in
hand.

Okonkwo's return to Umuofia is not really memorable. The clan
has undergone profound changes during his exile. The new religion, the new government, and the new trading stores are in
people's minds. Many see these institutions as evil, and most of
the villagers are not interested in Okonkwo's return. Okonkwo is
deeply grieved. He mourns for the whole clan, not just himself. He
sees the clan breaking up and falling apart. He mourns for the
warlike men of Umuofia who have become soft like women.

Mr. Brown discusses religion with Akunna, a respected elder in the Igbo community.

Analysis

Akunna explains the complex religious tradition of the Igbo. In this worldview, the creator God Chukwu is a remote masculine force. Chukwu is introduced in Part One of the novel as the creator God who teaches the people to survive through the cultivation of yams. The masculine Chukwu is balanced by lesser gods such as the feminine Earth goddess Ani and Agbala, the Oracle of the Hills and Caves. Chukwu is the supreme creator God; the lesser gods act as His messengers and relate to the daily lives of the Igbo people. One of Achebe's primary objectives in writing *Things Fall Apart* is to illustrate that the Igbo have a rich culture. In this chapter he shows that the Igbo believe in a Supreme God; they do not worship idols but understand the lesser gods who participate in their daily lives as manifestations of the Supreme God. Achebe exposes the truth about Igbo society, which once functioned as an organic whole where religion, government, social relationships, and the economy were connected. Traditional Igbo religion was the glue that held the Igbo culture together. Some critics interpret the conversation between Akunna and Mr. Brown as Achebe's search for convergence between the traditional and Christian religions.

Historically, the Christian missionaries offered the Igbo educational opportunities. The colonial powers subsidized the mission schools. As a result, Christianity became a handmaiden of the colonial government as education became an agent of Christianization. The results were double edged. As more and more Igbo took advantage of educational opportunities, they became Christians or synthesized Christianity with the traditional religion. However, as the Igbo assimilated Western culture, the traditional way of life fell apart.

Study Questions

1. What arguments does Akunna use to convince Mr. Brown that lesser gods act as messengers to Chukwu?

2. Why does Mr. Brown disapprove of Enoch's behavior?

3. What is Mr. Brown's attitude toward the traditional Igbo religion?

4. Akunna explains that the Igbo know Chukwu as the great creator god because many children are named Chukwuka. What does the name mean?

5. Why does Mr. Brown visit Okonkwo?

6. What is Nwoye's new Christian name?

7. How does Okonkwo respond to Mr. Brown's visit?

8. Why does Mr. Brown leave his mission?

9. Why does Okonkwo feel as though he has returned in the wrong year?

10. Describe Okonkwo's homecoming.

Answers

1. Akunna says that the lesser gods act as messengers to Chukwu just like Mr. Brown acts as a messenger of his church and the District Commissioner acts as a messenger of the ruler in England.

2. Mr. Brown disapproves of Enoch's action because he is over-zealous and provokes the clan. Enoch is the son of the snake cult's priest. He killed and ate a sacred python.

3. Mr. Brown respects the traditional Igbo religion.

4. The name Chukwuka means "Chukwu is Supreme."

5. Mr. Brown visits Okonkwo to tell him that he has just sent Okonkwo's son, Nwoye, to a new training college for teachers.

6. Nwoye's new Christian name is Isaac.

7. Okonkwo has Mr. Brown driven out of his homestead. He threatens to have him carried out if he comes again.

8. Mr. Brown leaves his mission because he is in poor health. He is very sorry to leave the people.

9. Okonkwo cannot initiate his sons in the *ozo* society immediately. He has to wait two years for the next round of initiation ceremonies.

10. Okonkwo's homecoming is disappointing to him. It is a nonevent to the rest of the villagers. The Igbo people are excited and concerned about the new religion, the new government, and the new economy. They are not concerned about Okonkwo.

Suggested Essay Topics

1. Okonkwo plans to return to Umuofia with a flourish. Discuss in detail three reasons why his return is not as exciting as he planned.

2. Explain one basic way in which the Igbo traditional religion is similar to Christianity. Explain another fundamental way in which the Igbo traditional religion is different from Christianity.

Chapter Twenty-Two

New Characters:

Reverend James Smith: *Mr. Brown's successor*

Okeke: *Mr. Smith's interpreter*

Ajofia: *the leading* egwugwu *of Umuofia*

Summary

Reverend Smith openly condemns Mr. Brown's policy of compromise, and he suspends a woman from the church who has allowed her heathen husband to mutilate her dead *ogbanje* child. Overzealous converts who smarted under Mr. Brown now flourish. Enoch, the son of the snake priest who is believed to have eaten the sacred python, sparks a great conflict between the church and clan in Umuofia. At the annual ceremony for the Earth goddess, the ancestors of the clan emerge as *egwugwu* through tiny antholes. Christian women who had gone to church could not go home because they could not pass the *egwugwu*. The men beg the spirits to retire so the women can pass. They are retiring when Enoch boasts that the *egwugwu* would not dare touch a Christian. One of them strikes Enoch with a cane; Enoch attacks him and tears off his mask. The other *egwugwu* immediately surround their desecrated companion and take him away. Enoch has killed an ancestral spirit, and Umuofia is thrown into confusion. That night the Mother of the Spirits walks throughout the clan weeping for her murdered son. It seems like the soul of the tribe is wailing for a great evil that is coming—its own death.

The next day, the masked *egwugwu* of Umuofia assemble in the marketplace. They include the dreadful Otakagu from Imo and Ekwensu from Uli. Bells clatter behind some of them, and the eerie voices of countless spirits are heard. For the first time, Mr. Smith is afraid and prays to be delivered from danger. The band of *egwugwu* move like a furious whirlwind and burn Enoch's compound to the ground. Then they go to the church intoxicated with destruction. When Mr. Smith sees the *egwugwu*, he nearly flees in fear. But instead, he walks toward them. Their bells clang, and their machetes clash. The air is full of dust and weird sounds.

Okeke, Mr. Smith's interpreter, is behind him. The *egwugwu* are surprised by their composure. Then, Ajofia, the leading *egwugwu* of Umuofia and the spokesman of the nine ancestors, rises up. As he speaks, clouds of smoke rise from his head. Mr. Smith looks at his interpreter, but Okeke is from Umuru, so he is at a loss too. Ajofia laughs at the ignorant strangers. He instructs the interpreter to tell Mr. Smith that the *egwugwu* liked the foolish Mr. Brown, and for his sake they will not harm Mr. Smith. However, he must go back to his house; the church will be destroyed because it has bred untold abominations. They say Mr. Smith may stay with the Igbo people and worship his own God if he agrees to follow their ways. Mr. Smith tells them his church is the house of God, and it should not be desecrated. In response, the *egwugwu* burn the red-earth church to the ground.

Analysis

The conflict between the Christian Igbo and the traditional Igbo clan is exacerbated by the intolerant Reverend Smith and the zealous convert Enoch. The *egwugwu* are symbols of the spirits of

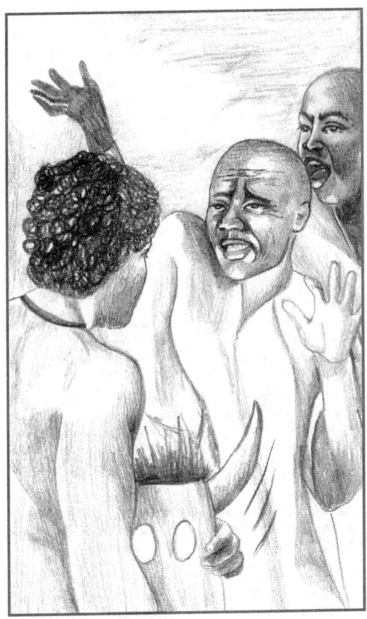

Enoch, the zealous convert, unmasks the traditional Igbo religion by unmasking an *egwugwu*.

the ancestors. When Enoch unmasks the *egwugwu*, he is committing an atrocity. His actions reveal that the elders and leaders are representing the spirits; some unbelievers would say the men are simply masquerading as spirits. The concept of the *egwugwu* is an integral part of the complex Igbo religious belief system and traditional worldview. By unmasking the *egwugwu*, Enoch symbolically kills the spirit of an ancestor; he also exposes the unmasked spirit to women, children, and men who are not yet initiated. This crime has never been committed in the history of Umuofia.

Christianity cuts into the core of Igbo life by striking at the traditional Igbo religion. As the spiral of history and human experience widens for the Igbo people through the age of European Imperialism, the foreigners put a knife in the traditional religion of the Igbo. Traditional religion holds the Igbo together; when it is undermined, the Igbo culture cannot hold. All things that are traditionally Igbo fall apart. The title of the novel comes from W. B. Yeats' poem "The Second Coming." The novel begins with a quote from the poem:

> Turning and turning in the widening gyre
> The falcon cannot hear the falconer;
> Things fall apart; the centre cannot hold;
> Mere anarchy is loosed upon the world.

A falcon is a hawk with long, pointed wings and a short, curved beak; it is trained to hunt small game. A falconer is a person who breeds, trains, or hunts with falcons. The image is a falcon turning and turning in a widening spiral so far away from the falconer that the bird cannot hear its trainer. He gets so far away that the line connecting him to the falconer cannot hold. The center snaps, and things fall apart. The result is chaos. The center that cannot hold in the Igbo world is the traditional religion. As Igbo life falls apart, the Igbo people are thrown into anarchy and chaos. The colonial era causes the African social order to disintegrate.

Study Questions

1. In Umuofia they say "as a man danced so the drums were beaten for him." (p. 131) How does this saying relate to Reverend Smith?

2. Why is Reverend Smith filled with wrath when he hears that a woman in the congregation allows her husband to mutilate her dead child?

3. Why do the villagers call Enoch "The Outsider who wept louder than the bereaved"? (p. 131)

4. What is the greatest crime a man can commit in Umuofia?

5. Why is Enoch disappointed to be hidden in the parsonage?

6. Why does Ajofia address Mr. Smith by saying, "The body of the white man, do you know me?" (p. 134)

7. Explain why Okeke is not on the best terms with Reverend Smith.

8. How does Reverend Smith feel about Okeke, his interpreter, as he stands by him confronting the angry spirits?

9. Explain how Okeke interprets Mr. Smith's words to the spirits and leaders of Umuofia.

10. Why is the spirit of the clan pacified by the action of the *egwugwu?*

Answers

1. The people said Reverend Smith dances a furious step; therefore, the drums go mad. They mean that Reverend Smith is an overzealous pastor who provokes anger among the traditional Igbo.

2. Reverend Smith believes the people are putting the old wine of the Igbo faith into the new wineskins of the Christian faith. One of his congregation has followed Igbo practices. A child was declared an *ogbanje,* who plagued its mother by dying and entering her womb to be born again four times. Then, it was mutilated to discourage it from returning.

3. Enoch's devotion to the new faith seems much greater than Mr. Brown's. Mr. Brown is moderate in his behavior, whereas Enoch is a zealot.

4. The greatest crime a man can commit in Umuofia is to unmask an *egwugwu* in public or do anything that might reduce its immortal prestige in the eyes of the uninitiated. This is exactly what Enoch did.

5. Enoch is disappointed to be hidden in the parsonage because he hopes a holy war is imminent. A few other Christians agree.

6. This is the language in which spirits speak to mortal men.

7. Okeke condemns Enoch's behavior at the meeting. He says Enoch should not be hidden in the parsonage because he will only draw the wrath of the clan on the pastor. Mr. Smith rebukes him in strong language and does not seek his advice after that.

8. Reverend Smith is deeply grateful to Okeke, his interpreter, for standing by him. He smiles with deep gratitude.

9. Okeke does not translate Mr. Smith's words exactly. Mr. Smith tells the *egwugwu* to leave the church. Okeke translates these words wisely by indicating that Mr. Smith is happy to have the *egwugwu* discuss their grievances.

10. The spirit of the clan is momentarily satisfied because the *egwugwu* burn the church to the ground.

Suggested Essay Topics

1. Compare and contrast Mr. Brown with Reverend Smith; compare and contrast Reverend Smith with Enoch.

2. Describe Enoch's crime and explain why it is such a serious offense.

Chapter Twenty-Three

Summary

For the first time in many years Okonkwo feels happy. Things seem to be getting back to normal. The clan that had turned false appears to be making amends. He speaks about violence, and his clansmen listen with respect. It is like the good old days when a warrior was a warrior. The clansmen do not agree to drive away the Christians, but they do agree to do something substantial. Nothing happens for two days after the destruction of the church. Yet, the men of Umuofia are armed because they do not want to be caught unaware like the men of Abame. The District Commissioner finally sends a sweet-talking messenger to the leaders of Umuofia asking them to meet in his headquarters. That is not strange; he often invited them to hold such discussions. The six leaders, including Okonkwo, arrive at the courthouse armed with machetes. The District Commissioner receives them politely, and they put down their arms. He wants to hear the Igbos' side of the story.

The interpreter leaves the courtroom and returns with 12 men. However, as one of the elders begins to tell the story about Enoch, there is a brief scuffle. It happens so quickly, the Igbo leaders do not have time to defend themselves. They are handcuffed and led into the guardroom. The commissioner explains that he will not harm them, but they must cooperate. He says that the British have brought a peaceful colonial administration so the Igbo people will be happy. However, they will not allow the Igbo to hurt one another. He indicates that the leaders will be released from prison as soon as a fine of 200 hundred bags of cowries is collected. The commissioner tells the court messengers to treat the men respectfully.

However, the leaders are not given food or water for two days, and they are not allowed to go outside to urinate or defecate. At night the court messengers taunt the prisoners and knock their shaven heads together. On the third day, the Igbo cannot withstand the hunger and insults. Okonkwo insists they should have killed the white man. The court messengers go to Umuofia to tell the

The leaders of Umuofia are locked in prison by the District Commissioner because they destroyed the Christians' church.

people that their leaders would not be released until they paid a fine of 250 bags of cowries. They say the leaders will be hanged in Umuru unless the fine is paid immediately.

Okonkwo's compound seems deserted. Everyone is speaking in whispers. Ezinma goes to Obierika, but he is not home. His wives think he has gone to a secret meeting. Ezinma is satisfied that something is being done. The men of Umuofia meet in the marketplace and collect 250 bags of cowries to appease the white man. They do not know that 50 bags will go to the court messengers, who had increased the fine.

Analysis

Okonkwo is comfortable with the traditional way of living. He is happy that the clan is finally going to defend itself, and he is glad to confront the District Commissioner. However, Okonkwo does not understand the white man's power. He does not realize that life has changed in Umuofia. He still believes that things will go back to normal if the white man is killed. As Okonkwo lacks understanding of the white man, the colonial government lacks understanding of Igbo beliefs, customs, and jurisprudence. The District Commissioner and the *kotma* provide a fictional representation of the colonial administration in Nigeria in the early twentieth century. The commissioner honestly believes that the powers of British Imperialism will be helpful to the Igbo people. He believes the administration will rescue these "primitive" people and restrain them from hurting one another. In addition to knowing nothing about Igbo life, he is unaware of the court messengers' behavior.

Historically, this chapter represents the "pacification" of the people of Nigeria as it occurred between 1900 and 1920. The Igbo living east and west of the Niger River spoke different dialects and developed different cultures and political systems. The decentralized Igbo were radically different from the Yoruba people in the southwest and the Hausa people in the north. Yet, the British conquerors forced these diverse people into a single nation through a "pacification" campaign. The British sought to "pacify" the Igbo by destroying their traditional religion and their way of life, by destroying entire villages, and by instituting a corrupt native court system that encouraged the Igbo of one area to oppress the Igbo of another area. The *kotma* in this chapter provide an example of the corruption rampant among the native court system. The words "primitive" and "pacification" are used with bitter irony at the end of the novel. The "pacification" and "civilization" of the British result in full scale violence illustrated by the destruction of Abame. In contrast, the ritual wars of the Igbo are relatively minor when a great warrior like Okonkwo claims five heads.

Study Questions

1. How does the District Commissioner coax the Igbo leaders?

2. What code of law does the District Commissioner use to judge the six Igbo leaders?

3. Why aren't the leaders of Umuofia suspicious when the District Commissioner invites them to the courthouse?

4. What pretense does the District Commissioner use to bring his 12 men into the talks with the Igbo leaders?

5. The District Commissioner tells his men to treat the leaders of Umuofia with respect. Describe how the court messengers humiliate the leaders.

6. How does Okonkwo react to the way the court messengers treat him?

7. How is the story of the detained leaders elaborated by the villagers?

8. Why is Umuofia described like a startled animal with erect ears, sniffing the silent air, and not knowing where to run after her leaders are imprisoned?

9. Why does Ezinma break her long visit to her future husband's family?

10. Why do the court messengers increase the fine from 200 bags of cowries to 250 bags of cowries?

Answers

1. The District Commissioner invites the leaders to talk like friends to ensure that the situation will not happen again.

2. The District Commissioner will administer justice according to the British code of law and "native" court system.

3. The men are not suspicious because the District Commissioner often calls the Igbo leaders together for discussions.

4. The District Commissioner says he wants his 12 men to hear the grievances of the Igbo leaders and take warning. He explains that many of his men come from distant places. Although they speak Igbo, they are ignorant of the customs of Umuofia.

5. One of the court messengers shaves off all the hair on the six leaders' heads while they are still handcuffed. They insult and beat the leaders.

6. Okonkwo is choked with hate.

7. Some villagers say the families of the imprisoned leaders will be hanged. Others say soldiers are ready to massacre the people of Umuofia.

8. Umuofia is described like a startled animal because it is a full moon, yet the children's voices are not heard on the playground. The women of Iguedo do not meet to learn their new dance, and young men who usually go abroad in moonlight stay home.

9. Ezinma returns home when she hears that her father has been imprisoned and is going to be hanged.

10. The court messengers increase the fine from 200 bags of cowries to 250 bags of cowries so they can skim 50 bags off the top of the fine. The people do not know that 50 bags will go directly to the court messengers.

Suggested Essay Topics

1. Describe Okonkwo's reaction to the summons from the District Commissioner and his reaction to his imprisonment.

2. Compare and contrast the way the District Commissioner and the court messengers treat the Igbo leaders.

Chapter Twenty-Four

New Characters:

Egonwanne: *a coward who moves the men of Umuofia to impotence*

Okika: *the first man to speak, one of those imprisoned*

Onyeka: *the man who salutes Umuofia first*

Summary

The leaders are released by the District Commissioner, who speaks about the Queen of England, peace, and the colonial government. The Igbo trudge home silently. Okonkwo's friends and family see the marks on his back where he has been whipped. Okonkwo swears vengeance on the white man's court. If Umuofia does not go to war, he will avenge himself. Okonkwo remembers the noblest war of the past, which was against Isike. Okudo was alive then; he was not a fighter, but his song turned every man into a lion. Isike was slaughtered, and Okonkwo believes, "Those were days when men were men." (p. 141)

Okonkwo feels Egonwanne is the biggest coward in Umuofia because he moves the Igbo men to impotence. Okonkwo is afraid he will say that the ancestors never fought a war of blame, and he vows to plan his own revenge if the men listen to Egonwanne. As people crowd into the marketplace, Onyeka salutes Umuofia with his booming voice. Then Okika, who is a great orator and one of those imprisoned, speaks. He explains that his father used to say, "Whenever you see a toad jumping in broad daylight, then know that something is after its life." (p. 143) He says something is after the life of the Igbo people. The gods like Idemili, Ogwugwu, and Agbala are weeping; the dead fathers are also weeping because of the shameful sacrilege and the abominations they have suffered. He laments that some Igbos are not present. The white men have broken the clan, and the Igbo have gone different ways. Some have joined the white man. If the people of Umuofia fight the stranger, they will shed the blood of clansmen. Okika says their forefathers never killed their brothers, but now loyal Igbo must turn on their clansmen. Okika says Eneke the bird was asked why he was always flying. He replied, "Men have learnt to shoot without missing their mark and I have learnt to fly without perching on a twig." (p. 144) He says the Igbo must root out the evil of the white man, and Igbo brothers who side with evil must be rooted out too.

Five court messengers arrive. Okonkwo springs to his feet and confronts the head messenger. The men of Umuofia are mute like a giant background of silent trees and giant creepers. The messenger says the white man has ordered the meeting to stop. Okonkwo draws his machete. The messenger crouches to avoid the blow, but Okonkwo swings. The messenger is decapitated; his head lays on the ground next to his body. Then the Igbo people come to life, and the meeting stops. Okonkwo looks at the dead man. He knows that Umuofia will not go to war because the people let the other messengers escape. Umuofia has broken into confusion instead of action. He senses terror in the tumult, and he hears the people say, "Why did he do it?" (p. 145) Okonkwo wipes his machete on the sand and walks away.

Analysis

Okonkwo intends to speak at the meeting but then chooses violent action over language, illustrating his inability to use words in moments of tension. Again, Okonkwo appears to be an impetuous, violent, and angry man paradoxically afraid of failure and doomed to failure in spite of his personal achievements and strong convictions. The clan of Umuofia has undergone profound change; nevertheless, Okonkwo clings to an ever weakening past. He resolves to reclaim the traditional power and authority usurped by the white man and murders the court messenger in an individualist act of vengeance. His clansmen are stunned and wonder why he did it. The people of Umuofia do not capture the other messengers because they are confused. The clan is not thinking, speaking, or acting in solidarity as it would have in the past. Okonkwo recognizes the failure of the clan to resist oppression and to respond to the rapid changes introduced by the British.

Okonkwo can be analyzed from various points of view in this chapter. The respect for the individual that allows a man to earn titles and become successful in the traditional Igbo world is abused by Okonkwo. The feminine elements of a balanced Igbo life are

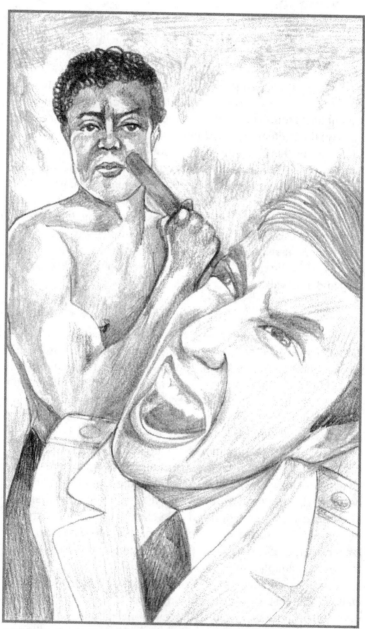

Okonkwo decapitates the District Commissioner's messenger at the meeting in the marketplace.

also denied by Okonkwo. Okonkwo violates the Week of Peace, takes a shot at his wife, participates in the ritual murder of Ikemefuna, and accidentally kills Ezeudu's son. Likewise, the clan throws twins away in the forest, ostracizes their mothers, enslaves the *osu*, and discriminates against unsuccessful men. The repressed feminine energies of Okonkwo gain force during Okonkwo's exile. In Part Two of the novel, Okonkwo is forced to take refuge within the feminine principle; in Umuofia, twins are rescued, their abject mothers, the *osu*, and weak men are given dignity and new life through Christianity. However, as Christianity gives voice to the disenfranchised, it simultaneously destroys traditional life, divides the clan, and introduces a violent colonial government.

Okonkwo only understands the strengths of Igbo life. He relates to the masculine energies and does not understand the feminine energies of the Igbo experience. Okonkwo defends himself and the traditional way of life. He upholds the Igbo concepts of communalism, equal opportunity, strong kinship relationships, and the traditional religion. However, he does not question the injustices of traditional life such as the Igbos' treatment of twins, discrimination against the *osu*, and the marginalization of the weak and abnormal. The traditional order fragments when the community is challenged by Christianity—the new faith that unmasks the *egwugwu* and survives in the Evil Forest. The new religion weakens Igbo society; as a result, things fall apart, and the clan cannot resist colonial injustice.

Okonkwo may be representative of the fundamental Igbo attitude of individualism and independence. He may also be a microcosm for the traditional Igbo worldview. Okonkwo is a paradoxical protagonist. Although Achebe has created an entirely fictional character and setting, the narrative recreates Igbo history. The denouement happens so swiftly, the reader must reread the chapter to confirm that Okonkwo did in fact decapitate the court messenger. The ending of the novel descends as quickly and forcibly as colonial rule descended upon the Igbo people.

Study Questions

1. Why are the women and children afraid to welcome the leaders home?

2. What are the long stripes on Okonkwo's back?

3. Why does Okonkwo have trouble sleeping that night?

4. Why does Okonkwo refer to the war with Isike saying, "Those were days when men were men"? (p. 141)

5. What does Okonkwo mean when he says he would show Egonwanne his back and his head if he talks about a war of blame?

6. Why does Okonkwo grind his teeth?

7. What does Okika mean when he says, "Whenever you see a toad jumping in broad daylight, then know that something is after its life"? (p. 143)

8. Okika says Eneke the bird was asked why he is always flying. He replied "Men have learnt to shoot without missing their mark and I have learnt to fly without perching on a twig." (p. 144) What is the meaning of the proverb, and how does it apply to the novel?

9. Why does Okonkwo decapitate the court messenger?

10. Why don't the people of Umuofia support Okonkwo and capture the other four messengers?

Answers

1. The leaders walk silently with heavy and fearsome looks on their faces.

2. The long stripes on Okonkwo's back are the marks left by the whip.

3. Okonkwo is excited about the meeting planned for the next day.

4. Okonkwo believes that men were brave in the past. The glorious war with Isike is an example.

5. Okonkwo means he would show Egonwanne his shaved head and the marks of the whip on his back.

6. Okonkwo grinds his teeth because he is so angry.

7. Okika means that something is after the life of the Igbo people.

8. The proverb means that Eneke the bird learned how to adapt and protect himself. Because men were not missing their targets when they shot, he learned how to keep on flying and not perch on a twig. If he did perch on a twig, he might be shot. Eneke the bird learned how to adapt. Perhaps Okika means the Igbo people must learn to adapt like Eneke.

9. Okonkwo decapitates the court messenger because he is so angry. He wants to fight, and he will not listen to the messenger who tries to stop the meeting of Umuofia.

10. The people of Umuofia are confused and frightened when Okonkwo decapitates the court messenger. They do not know what to do.

Suggested Essay Topics

1. Give three basic reasons why Okonkwo kills the court messenger. Use examples to support your points.

2. Give three basic reasons why the people of Umuofia do not rise up and support Okonkwo by capturing the other four messengers. Use examples to support your points.

Chapter Twenty-Five

Summary

Some of the men of Umuofia are sitting in Okonkwo's *obi* when the District Commissioner arrives. They tell him that Okonkwo is not present. The commissioner becomes angry and he says he will lock them all up if they do not produce Okonkwo. Obierika says they will take him to Okonkwo; perhaps the commissioner will be able to help them. The commissioner is annoyed at the way the Igbo use superfluous words. The District Commissioner is armed, and he warns Obierika that he and his men will be shot if he pulls any tricks.

The men lead the commissioner into a small bush behind Okonkwo's compound. They come to the tree from which Okonkwo's body is hanging. Obierika explains that perhaps the commissioner's men could take Okonkwo down and bury him. The District Commissioner changes from a resolute administrator to a student of "primitive" customs. He asks why the men cannot take Okonkwo down themselves. They explain it is against Igbo custom because it is an abomination for a man to take his own life. Suicide is an offense against the Earth, and any man who commits suicide cannot be buried by his clansmen because his body is evil. Only strangers can bury him. Then the Igbo will make sacrifices to cleanse the desecrated land.

As Obierika gazes at his friend's dangling body, he bitterly says that Okonkwo was one of the greatest men in Umuofia. The white man drove him to kill himself, and now he will be buried like a dog. The District Commissioner orders his men to cut down the body and take the corpse and all the people present to court. The District Commissioner has had much experience, and he believes he is bringing civilization to Africa. The commissioner plans to write a book about the Igbo people. He feels the story about Okonkwo, the man who killed a court messenger and then hanged himself, will make interesting reading. He thinks he could almost write a whole chapter on him. Then he reconsiders, perhaps the story only merits a paragraph. He has decided to title his book "The Pacification of the Primitive Tribes of the Lower Niger." (p. 148)

Analysis

Okonkwo is a paradox. He seems to represent traditional Igbo life, yet his self-destruction contradicts everything the Igbo society represents. Okonkwo cannot resist the white man and the forces of European Imperialism alone. Foreign Africans support the colonial order, and Igbo institutions are ineffective. The traditional world has been destroyed, and Okonkwo does not want to live in a new world. Okonkwo may be a tragic hero because as he stands for his convictions, his individualism results in disaster. He realizes that his efforts to save the traditional world are futile. His suicide saves him imprisonment, cheats the whites of revenge, and makes a mockery of the values of the clan. Is Okonkwo mad? What

Even though Okonkwo commits suicide, Obierika says he was one of the greatest men in Umuofia.

does he really stand for and what is the significance of his destruction? Does Okonkwo represent the suicidal fragmentation of Igbo society? Okonkwo's life is ruled by fear of failure. Yet, Okonkwo fails. He is unable to understand his father or son; he is unable to balance the male and female energies in the traditional world order, and he is unable to adapt to the changes introduced by the white colonizer. Okonkwo's suicide is shocking and ambiguous; ironically, his death is as shameful as his father's. His friend Obierika again provides invaluable insight and a reliable picture of the collapse of traditional life. He understands that Christianity has put a knife on the things that held the Igbo together. In his bitter epitaph for Okonkwo he addresses the District Commissioner saying, "That man was one of the greatest men in Umuofia. You drove him to kill himself; and now, he will be buried like a dog . . . " (p. 147)

The District Commissioner provides an ironic foil to Okonkwo. He believes he is bringing peace and civilization to the Igbo people, but in fact he has systematically destroyed many aspects of Igbo life. He trivializes the tragedy of Okonkwo and the conflict between the European and Igbo cultures by planning to summarize Okonkwo's struggle in one paragraph in his book, "The Pacification of the Primitive Tribes of the Lower Niger." The commissioner's title alludes to the imposition of British authority through separate conquests of individual Igbo communities. Perhaps "The Annihilation of the Socially Cohesive Ethnic Groups of the Lower Niger" would be a better title for his book.

Finally, in his foreword to Charles Larson's *Emergence of African Fiction*, Newton Stallknecht states, "Achebe describes, often with shrewd anthropological insight, the moral disintegration of an ancestral order and of an heroic leader brought into collision with European powers and ideas." (x–xi) Yet, the reader must understand the text as more than a basic ethnography. Achebe's *Things Fall Apart* is a novel; the text is a fictional representation of the past; it is not history. Achebe attempts to present positive and negative aspects of traditional Igbo life without idealizing or romanticizing the past. He succeeds in painting a portrait of the ordered and civil Igbo society. Indeed, the story of Okonkwo affirms that Europe did not introduce civilization to savages.

Study Questions

1. Is Okonkwo's suicide entirely unexpected?

2. Why does Obierika send for strangers from another village?

3. Why does Obierika ask the commissioner to bury Okonkwo's body?

4. Why is suicide such an abomination among the Igbo?

5. Why is Obierika so angry at the District Commissioner?

6. Why does the District Commissioner think he is bringing civilization to the Igbo people?

7. How does the District Commissioner trivialize the great tragedy of Okonkwo?

8. Explain why the title of the District Commissioner's book is ironic.

9. Why do you think Okonkwo hung himself?

10. Why does Achebe have Okonkwo hang himself "off stage"?

Answers

1. Okonkwo's suicide happens very quickly offstage. The reader may not be aware of what is happening at first. However, Okonkwo's suicide has been foreshadowed throughout the novel. Refer to pages 17, 95, and 100 of the text.

2. Obierika sends for strangers to cut down and bury Okonkwo. The Igbo cannot bury Okonkwo because he has committed suicide.

3. Obierika has sent for strangers from another village, but he is afraid it will be a long time before they arrive. He asks the District Commissioner to bury Okonkwo instead.

4. Suicide is an offense against the Earth goddess.

5. Obierika is Okonkwo's best friend. He says that Okonkwo was one of the greatest men in Umuofia. The white man drove him to kill himself, and he will be buried like a dog.

6. The District Commissioner does not understand Igbo life or customs. By imposing the British worldview, he feels he is helping the people.

7. The District Commissioner trivializes the great tragedy of Okonkwo by allotting his story only one paragraph in his book about the Igbo.

8. The title of the District Commissioner's book is "The Pacification of the Primitive Tribes of the Lower Niger." The title is ironic because the British did not bring peace to the people; they brought violence and conflict.

9. Perhaps Okonkwo hung himself because the Igbo people did not rise up in support of him. He could not resist the white man alone. He did not want to be arrested and subjected to prison and humiliation again.

10. Classic tragic heroes deal with disaster "offstage." Achebe may have Okonkwo hang himself "offstage" because he wants the reader to understand Okonkwo as a classic tragic hero.

Suggested Essay Topics

1. Is Okonkwo a tragic hero, or is he a fool? Is Okonkwo selfish? How would you describe Okonkwo at the end of the novel? Use three examples to support your point.

2. What does the title of the District Commissioner's book tell you about his attitude toward the Igbo people? How would a successful Igbo living in Umuofia at the time of Okonkwo's death title the commissioner's book? How would an *osu* or an anguished mother of twins title the work? How would you title the commissioner's book?

SECTION FIVE

Sample Analytical Paper Topics

Topic #1

Discuss the significance of *Things Fall Apart* as a social document and a novel dramatizing traditional Igbo life and its first encounter with colonialism and Christianity at the turn of the twentieth century.

Outline

I. Thesis Statement: Things Fall Apart *recreates the conflict between European and Igbo cultures at the turn of the twentieth century by focusing on the cataclysmic changes introduced by the forces of colonialism and Christianity.*

II. Social and Economic Life of the Igbo

    A. Social structure of the Igbo

    B. Role of men and women

    C. Role of marriage and the family

    D. Significance of the yam

III. Traditional Politics

    A. Umuofia and the political structure

    B. Success and personal achievement

    C. The title-taking system

    D.   The leadership role of elders

    E.   The judicial role of *egwugwu*

IV. Colonial Changes in Economic and Political Life

    A.   Significance of the palm-oil trade

    B.   The colonial administration

    C.   The District Commissioner

    D.   The native court

    E.   The role of court messengers

V.   Traditional Igbo Religion

    A.   Chukwu, the Supreme Creator God

    B.   Ani, the Earth goddess

    C.   Agbala, and the Oracles

    D.   Ritual sacrifices

    E.   The feminine and masculine principles

    F.   *Ogbanje* children

    G.   The abandonment of twins

    H.   The role of the ancestors

    I.   Titles and reincarnation

    J.   Children and reincarnation

VI. Christianity and Changes in Social and Religious Life

    A.   The missionary factor

    B.   The first Igbo Christians: *osu*, mothers of twins, unsuccessful men

    C.   Zealots

    D.   Conflicts with traditional beliefs

    E.   Breakup of the Igbo clan

VII. The Author's Recreation of History through Literary Techniques (Optional)

    A.   Characterization of Okonkwo

    B.   Use of proverbs

    C.   Use of stories within the text

    D.   Significance of the title in relationship to "The Second Coming"

VIII. Conclusion

    A.   The use of literature to record history

    B.   The author's purpose and point of view

Topic #2

Prove that Okonkwo, a talented Igbo who strives to succeed in the traditional world, is a microcosm of Igbo society because he is destroyed by internal and external forces.

Outline

I.   Thesis Statement: *Like Igbo society at the turn of the century, Okonkwo is destroyed by internal and external forces. He is inflexible and unable to balance the masculine and feminine principles of traditional Igbo life, and he resists the external forces of European Imperialism and Christianity.*

II.   Okonkwo

    A.   Desire to succeed

    B.   Fear of failure

    C.   Comparison with Unoka and Nwoye

III. Okonkwo's Inability to Balance Feminine and Masculine Energies

    A.   Crimes against the Earth Goddess

        1.   Treatment of Ojiugo during the Week of Peace

        2.   Treatment of Ekwefi during the new Yam Festival

        3.   Participation in Ikemefuna's ritual murder

        4.   Accidental killing of Ezeudu's son

    B.   Exile

        1.   Superficial understanding of the concept "Mother is
             Supreme"

        2.   Determination to succeed through hard work

    C.   Alienation of Nwoye

IV. Conflict with European Imperialism and Christianity

    A.   Hatred of Christians

    B.   Conflict with Reverend Smith

    C.   Conflict with native court

    D.   Decapitation of court messenger

V.   Tensions within Igbo Society

    A.   Title-taking system measuring success

    B.   Ritual sacrifice

    C.   Abandonment of twins

    D.   Treatment of *osu*

    E.   Banishment for involuntary manslaughter

VI. Impact of Christianity and European Imperialism

    A.   Marginalized Igbos become Christian

    B.   Native courts hold power

VII. Conclusion

    A.   Okonkwo is destroyed by self and external forces

    B.   Igbo society falls apart due to internal tensions and ex-
         ternal forces

    C.   Okonkwo is a microcosm of Igbo society at the turn of
         the twentieth century

Topic #3

Prove that Okonkwo is a tragic hero. Explain how Okonkwo
encompasses the pathos of a culture undergoing cataclysmic
change. How does Okonkwo's story evoke both pity and fear? Analyze Okonkwo's tragic flaw and subsequent downfall.

Outline

I.　Thesis Statement: *Okonkwo achieves the stature of a tragic hero, evokes both pity and fear, and suffers a downfall because of his fear of failure, his inflexibility in living traditional Igbo life, and his inability to adapt to new ideas.*

II.　Heroic Stature

　　A.　Physical strength and appearance

　　B.　Personal achievements

　　C.　Success: Material wealth, titles, prestige

　　D.　Leadership in the clan

　　E.　Drive to achieve immortality and take the highest titles in the land

III.　Pity

　　A.　Mediocre *chi*

　　B.　Fear of failure

　　C.　Contrast with Unoka and Nwoye

　　D.　Inability to express love

　　E.　Inability to balance the masculine and feminine energies in Igbo life

　　F.　Accidental killing of Ezeudu's son

　　G.　Exile in Mbanta

IV.　Disapproval

　　A.　Harsh treatment of wives and children

　　B.　Ritual murder of Ikemefuna

　　C.　Alienation of Nwoye

　　D.　Anger against the Christians

　　E.　Anger against the white men

　　F.　Violent decapitation of court messenger

V.   Tragic Flaw

   A.   Inability to balance feminine and masculine energies

   B.   Inflexibility in living traditional Igbo life

   C.   Inability to adapt to new ideas

VI. Downfall

   A.   Destabilization of Okonkwo and Igbo institutions by colonial powers

   B.   Inability to unite the Igbo people against the white man

   C.   Inability to save Igbo life and culture from falling apart

   D.   Suicide

   E.   Burial

   F.   Reduction to paragraph in commissioner's book

VII. Conclusion

   A.   Comparison of Okonkwo to Ikemefuna, sensitive musician and hunter

   B.   Comparison of Okonkwo to Ezeudu, the revered elder

   C.   Comparison of Okonkwo to Obierika, his balanced friend

SECTION SIX

Bibliography

Quotations from *Things Fall Apart* are taken from the following edition:

Achebe, Chinua. *Things Fall Apart*. Portsmouth, NH: Heinemann, 1996.

The following works were also cited or consulted:

Achebe, Chinua. *Morning Yet on Creation Day*. Portsmouth, NH: Heinemann, 1996.

Innes, C. L. and Bernth Lindfors, eds. *Critical Perspectives on Chinua Achebe*. London: Heinemann, 1979.

Isichei, Elizabeth. *A History of the Igbo People*. New York: St. Martin's Press, 1976.

Killam, G. D. *The Novels of Chinua Achebe*. New York: Africana Publishing House, 1969.

Larson, Charles R. *The Emergence of African Fiction*. Bloomington: Indiana University Press, 1971.

Lindfors, Bernth, ed. *Approaches to Teaching Achebe's Things Fall Apart*. New York: Modern Language Association of America, 1991.

Ohadike, Don C. *Anioma: A Social History of the Western Igbo People*. Athens: Ohio University Press, 1994.

Ohadike, Don C. "Igbo Culture and History" in Chinua Achebe. *Things Fall Apart*. Portsmouth, NH: Heinemann, 1996. (xix-xlix)

Uchendu, Victor C. *The Igbo of Southeast Nigeria*. New York: Holt, Rinehart and Winston, 1965.

Wren, Robert. *Achebe's World: The Historical and Cultural Context of the Novels of Chinua Achebe*. Harlow, England: Longman Studies in African Literature, 1981.

MAXnotes®

REA's Literature Study Guides

MAXnotes® are student-friendly. They offer a fresh look at masterpieces of literature, presented in a lively and interesting fashion. **MAXnotes®** offer the essentials of what you should know about the work, including outlines, explanations and discussions of the plot, character lists, analyses, and historical context. **MAXnotes®** are designed to help you think independently about literary works by raising various issues and thought-provoking ideas and questions. Written by literary experts who currently teach the subject, **MAXnotes®** enhance your understanding and enjoyment of the work.